LODGE SPIRIT

RALPH M. KNEALE, JR.

LODGE SPIRIT

A BRIEF HISTORY OF NATURE APPRECIATION IN AMERICA

plus An Insider's View of Look About Lodge

TATE PUBLISHING
AND ENTERPRISES, LLC

Published by Tate Publishing & Enterprises, LLC
127 E. Trade Center Terrace | Mustang, Oklahoma 73064 USA
1.888.361.9473 | www.tatepublishing.com

Tate Publishing is committed to excellence in the publishing industry. The company reflects the philosophy established by the founders, based on Psalm 68:11,
"The Lord gave the word and great was the company of those who published it."

Published in the United States of America

ISBN: 978-1-61862-395-9
1. HISTORY/United States/State & Local/Midwest
2. NATURE/Environmental Conservation & Protection
12.11.14

Table of Contents

Dedication

This book is dedicated to the many people who imbued and enhanced in me, and in many others, a true love of nature. These influences include, but are certainly not limited to:

My parents;

Ralph M. Kneale, early Boy Scout leader, Science Club Life Member, engineer, and lifelong lover of nature.
Katherine F. Kneale, the consumate *green thumb* gardner of flowers and vegetables, and also a noted dietition, cook, and resturant owner. In addition, she was also a lifelong lover of nature.

Many Cleveland Natural Science Club members, including:

Edna Hopp Doller, early Club member (joined 1925) and dedicated teacher of the natural sciences.
Edward W. Doller, early Club member (joined 1931), engineer, and key contributor to the Lodge's building, maintenance, and operation.
Ellis C. Persing, noted natural science professor, Club founder, and an inspiration to many.

And definitely not last, my son:

Todd D. Kneale, skilled Yosemite hiker who introduced his parents to, and then hiked them through, John Muir's world.

Contributions—from Many People

Creating this volume has been a labor of love, plus an assumed obligation, based on my early experiences in and around Look About Lodge. In a more important sense, it is documentation of a special part of Greater Cleveland's (and our country's) and natural history. As part of the background that led to the building of today's Look About Lodge, I offer insights on how Northeast Ohio embraced nature appreciation and conservation with Cleveland Metroparks in the early 1900s.

These writings are provided to honor the many early Science Club members who brought nature appreciation to the lives of so many people. They gave an enduring love of the natural sciences to me and numerous others! I hope this volume will, in some small way, have a similar affect on you and your family.

My parents were dedicated nature lovers. While the records show that they became members of The Cleveland Natural Science Club in 1938 (the year of the new Lodge's dedication), a number of their close friends and college classmates were earlier members of The Science Club. This included Edna Hopp and Ed Doller[1] (Ed and Eddy as they were called) who also functioned as a surrogate aunt and uncle to me.

Some of the early Science Club historians who spent hours clipping articles, saving documents, and making scrapbooks have made this volume possible. Several scrapbook binders were used to compile Bulletins and other documents[2]. Many historical records and photos have been lost or discarded. Fortunately, a number of nature lovers who respect history saved and/or found the materials that exist today[3], and that I have used to make this book factual.

The most recent and current contributors include:

Ann Burgess, Club historian who wrote a history of the Club and the Lodges for the new Look About Lodge's twenty-fifth anniversary on September 21, 1963.

Frances Adelaide Lennie Snider, also a Science Club historian, who presented a history of the Club at its fiftieth anniversary on May 18th, 1974.[4]

Jeanne Furst, who served as Science Club president, newsletter writer, program chairperson, and historian before her passing in 2005.

Wendy Weirich, MEd, Naturalist Manager of Look About Lodge from 1993 to 2008. Wendy developed a passionate love of this special building.

As the first naturalist manager of the Lodge after it was transferred from the Cleveland Natural Science Club to Cleveland Metroparks, she created a PowerPoint photo presentation on the history of the Lodge. This has been continually updated and presented to numerous audiences throughout the years.

Wendy also accomplished getting Look About Lodge listed on the US Register of Historic Places.

Sandra Cobb, MLS, a special-libraries librarian who did most of the archival research for the National Register application on a volunteer basis.

Mack Bell, Alice Kruse, and Robert Hinkle who invested many hours in editing and proofreading.

Introduction

"History tells us why we are who we are."

History Channel

This book was written to provide an insider's view of Look About Lodge, from its creation to its culmination as a unique nature education center. The Lodge is loved by staff and visitors alike.

I begin with a brief history of nature appreciation in America. Then I document the formation of Cleveland Natural Science Club and the growth of Cleveland Metroparks. These are the partners that created Look About Lodge and made it what it is today – a unique nature education facility that instills a love of nature and the natural sciences in literally thousands of people annually.

The historical photos were all taken in the 1930s and 1940s, and scanned for reproduction. They are not of ideal quality, but they were included because of their unique content.

An appreciation of and a love for nature is a rewarding gift. It is hoped that this volume can help you and those you influence to become more enriched from the rewards nature offers. It is my response to Ernest Thompson Seton's counsel, "You must, in some sort, note it down and pass it on to another way-seeker."

I write this work down because I am apparently the last legacy of those who were early Science Club members and spent time at Look About Lodge in the 1930s and 1940s. It is a story that needs to be documented, because it is an important part of Greater Cleveland's history. I consider it my responsibility to "note it down and pass it on."

This is the story of today's Look About Lodge, supported by an overview of our country's commitment to nature appreciation. Section I introduces you to the Cleveland Natural Science Club, which created Look About Lodge. Sections II and III put the club's founding in the context of the nature appreciation movement. Section IV covers the details of the Look About Lodges. Section V describes the life and activities of the Club behind Look About Lodge, and then Section VI is a timeline to tie it all together.

Today's Look About Lodge is an enchanting place in which to receive nature enrichment. It was designed as a clubhouse with two purposes. First, it was a base from which to study and to educate others about nature. In addition, it was also a retreat in which to commune with nature.

Today's medical science has determined that nature enriches a person by allowing the release of tension and a feeling of enjoyment. Think about this next time you go for a walk in the woods. Doesn't it refresh you and make you forget your problems and cares?

One question we might ask is, "What prompted the interest in nature and conservation in the early nineteen hundreds?" We will never know for sure, but it's a pretty good guess that the naturalists of the 1800s played a key role. It was during the late 1800s that Seton, Muir, Thoreau, Burroughs and others began promoting the benefits of preserving our wildernesses. This led to an awareness of and interest in nature by much of the American public. This interest was enhanced by Theodore Roosevelt and embraced by many.

I surmise that the most logical answer as to what prompted this country's interest in nature and conservation is that it was motivated by John Muir and Ernest Thompson Seton and enhanced by the writings of John Burroughs.

"In 1900, a wilderness craze was sweeping the country. Hiking and mountaineering were in fashion. The Audubon Society and the Sierra Club had recently been formed. People were fleeing the cities, heading for 'the great outdoors.'"

The return to nature was widespread in the early 1900s. People living in cities decided that they had lost something, and they wanted it back. What they had lost was the real wilderness. They wanted to pack up and go camping overnight and to climb serious mountains, as compared to the much smaller mountains we have in the East.

For the first time, people began talking about nature conservation. Muir saw in "the back to nature" craze recruits for his campaign to preserve the wilderness. "Even the scenery habit in its most artificial forms," he wrote, "mixed with spectacles, silliness, and Kodiaks, its devotees arrayed more gorgeously than scarlet tanagers, even this is encouraging, and may well be a hopeful sign of the times."

Muir saw the good side of this and was an optimist, so he found reason for hope.

In 1900, America boasted five national parks; and there were still millions of acres of untouched wilderness. The environmental movement Muir championed found support in Washington. That year, Congress, for the first time, passed legislation protecting wildlife that was in danger of extinction, and, the Senate finally moved to protect the buffalo. At that time, there were only four hundred left on the entire continent.

The founding Science Club members were educators who had chosen to include the natural sciences as part of their teaching career. As I studied Ernest Thompson Seton, with whom I was already somewhat familiar, more extensively it proved to be very enlightening. And then there was John Muir, whom I learned about later in my life. It was interesting to note that both of these naturalists had done quite a bit of writing.

Because birds are the most prevalent examples of nature for many people, I also looked into the life of John Audubon. He, too, recognized the need to set aside land for wildlife habitat and nature preservation. As an artist, Audubon undoubtedly influenced those who were youngsters in the first two decades of the 1900s. John Bartram was important to the botanical history of our country, so I delved a little into his background as well.

Thus, I offer the brief histories of these naturalists as background or context into why the Science Club and then Look About Lodge came into being. If you are interested in nature—and why else would you be reading this book—I think you will find these men's stories interesting.

Like John Burroughs, the inclination to write came to me well after childhood. In my case the proclivity was practical—writing technical literature and marketing materials for manufacturers—while John Burroughs was truly inspirational.

Among other challenges in school, I disliked memorizing dates in history. So it is with somewhat of an apology that I have included numerous dates in this volume. This was done to provide reference points in the development of nature appreciation, the Cleveland Natural Science Club, and Look About Lodge.

I hereby direct that if any student reads this book for an academic purpose, the teacher is not to take off any credit for dates not remembered.

This compilation of facts and memories on Look About Lodge and nature appreciation began with "Notes From The Past," reflections that were written for the Cleveland Natural Science Club's 81st Anniversary Dinner in May of 2004. An excerpt from those "Notes" follows:

Notes From The Past

Some of my most vivid, and pleasant, memories are of my early years at Look About Lodge during the 1940s. I also enjoyed outings to many of the Cleveland Metroparks reservations, including the South Chagrin, North Chagrin, and Euclid Creek (we called it Bluestone) Reservations. Throughout my life, I have thought frequently about The Lodge and the events that gave me a love of nature.

As a kid, I drank in the atmosphere—the smell of the hemlocks, the ever-present aroma of chestnut logs, the sounds of the owls at night, and song birds during the day. I regret that

as an enthusiastic kid, I was so mesmerized by the moods that I didn't form more detailed memories of the activities that the Lodge was built to house.

From the perspective of an elder, it is perhaps easier to understand the present by knowing what—and who—went before. Such knowledge can enrich your own experiences, enhance your appreciation, and expand your enjoyment of life!

These notations on Look About Lodge and The Cleveland Natural Science Club are provided by one who lived through, and was enriched by, many of the early years. I hope they will enrich your life a little. May these memories give you, a nature-loving Lodge visitor, a better understanding of this special place!

I regret not consistently following the counsel of John Burroughs[5]. So, I recommend his advice to all:

"I come here often to find myself. It is so easy to get lost in the world!"

It is unfortunate that my generation, the children of The Cleveland Natural Science Club's founders and early members, didn't do more to avoid being the "Last Child In The Woods."[6] I ask that you respect this building's history by leaving your impressions, and your photos, so others can be inspired!

May these notations on Look About Lodge and The Cleveland Natural Science Club enrich your experiences in this unique sanctuary. And, may they enhance the spirit of nature appreciation and conservation in you plus others whom you influence.

A New Theory of Relativity

When you ask almost any American to name their favorite or most admired sports figure, most would have a ready answer. When you can ask any American to name their most admired naturalist, and they can give an answer, then we will be close to giving nature the awareness and respect it deserves.

In my recent adult life, I would probably name John Muir first. That's because Muir came into my life about two decades ago during our family's first trip to Yosemite National Park, and he was ever present during our three successive trips there.

I would also name Ernest Thompson Seton. He was among the first to kindle my nature appreciation. The date noted inside the cover of my *Lives of the Hunted* [7] (which was my father's) is Thanksgiving, 1901.

Wild Animals I Have Known and *Lives of the Hunted* were two books that had a strong impact on my childhood. They provided keen insight into the world of nature and wild animals that was of great interest.

Most children in Greater Cleveland would name the naturalist of their closest Cleveland Metroparks nature center as their favorite. That's because that naturalist impressed them with a hands-on knowledge of nature that is not readily available in a normal classroom curriculum, or from most parents.

In Greater Cleveland, and in the eastern counties of Lake and Geauga, most children visit a park system during the course of their school studies. Many children also attend Park System or Natural History Museum sponsored programs with their parents.

We in Greater Cleveland are not unique in having parks and a museum of natural history. We are, however, unique in the quality and accessibility of these institutions.

Research from many sources has been used to compile this book. Since writing *Notes from the Past* over six years ago, my memories and understanding of the Lodge have been enhanced by reading the historical documents that remain from the early years of the Cleveland Natural Science Club. My sentiments and gratitude for my appreciation of nature have been. enhanced.

Both my academic and experiential education validate that knowing a person's background is key to understanding that person. Thus, in this book, I have included the significant facts about some of the people known to be major influences on nature appreciation, and who probably influenced the builders of the inspirational place we call Look About Lodge.

As noted in the introduction to Section III, the Washarn-Langford-Doane Expedition that led to the establishment of Yellowstone National Park was financed by its members. It is interesting that the building and furnishing of today's Look About Lodge was also financed by the Cleveland Natural Science Club membership, albeit with help from a WPA grant.

It can also be argued that the early educational efforts of the Cleveland Natural Science Club inspired today's nationally recognized and award winning Cleveland Metroparks Outdoor Education Program.

As elders, we frequently reflect on our earlier experiences. The emotions imbued in my early years from the influence of Science Club members and the atmosphere of Look About Lodge have grown stronger. I am grateful that circumstances have allowed me to return to the Lodge and gather more facts about the building and the organization that so heavily influenced my formative years.

In this volume, I offer my experiences and insights on the Lodge, plus insights into who and what led to the creation of the Lodge. As apparently the last known living legacy of the Lodge's early years, I hope this information will help foster a fresh nature awakening in you, your family, and your friends.

If you haven't already done so, please visit Look About Lodge. Call first; it's not always open—440-247-7075. It offers an inspiring atmosphere from which to commune with, and to study, nature. The Lodge surrounds you with the rustic atmosphere of the logs from which it was built. You may still be able to smell the chestnut fragrance that was so predominant seventy plus years ago. You should definitely walk along the hemlock-lined trail that borders the Lodge to the south.

You can admire the lawn in front of the east porch that gently slopes down to the woods. You can also enjoy the lawn that extends to the west, and maybe even have a bite to eat at the picnic tables by the four-sided fireplace that are just beyond the west lawn.

Some Impressionable Influences

Examples of how you can impart the reward of nature appreciation

The influences in my life included Cleveland Natural Science Club field trips, such as the annual visit to a sugar bush. For me, this lead to the annual tapping of the two maple trees in our front yard. We used large tin cans to gather the sap, and then boiled it on the stove into (somewhat expensive, but educational) maple syrup.

Maybe more important were the walks along the hemlock-lined trail above the Sulphur Springs gorge, and down the vegetation lined nature trail to the creek at the bottom. And, of course, just sitting in the wide-armed Adirondack chairs of the assembly room, listening to the songbirds singing and the trees rustling during the day, or hearing the owls and otherwise refreshing silence of the night hours made a lasting impression on me.

Most people with a love of nature have a childhood memory that had a strong impact on their lives. For me, in addition to my time at Look About Lodge, it was the family vacation taken when I was just five.

We went to a cabin in Northern Minnesota (where my parents had spent their honeymoon). It was located on a series of lakes in Eagle's Nest Minnesota. This is the same region of the Gofer State that inspired Jim Brandenburg to write *Brother Wolf: A Forgotten Promise*.[8]

The cabin was miles from "civilization." We fished from a rowboat and ate the catch for lunch or supper. It was a relatively small cabin, so I slept at one end of the screened-in porch that stretched across the cabin's front. Deer would often nuzzle the screen next to my bed. This prompted me to leave dried fruit and other treats outside the porch before I went to bed. Even in 1940, these mystic animals were looking for a handout!

As a pre-teen, my parents and I would spend a week in the summer and weekends in the spring and fall at Look About Lodge as a member host family. We would also come to the South or North Chagrin Reservations of Cleveland Metroparks for breakfasts, lunches, or suppers. The Euclid Creek Reservation (we called it Bluestone) was another favorite destination for outings and picnics, some of which we attended with fellow Science Club members.

Another major influence in my—and my wife's—nature appreciation was our son, Todd. Todd took an outdoor leadership class in high school, which included a trip to the Allegheny foothills of Pennsylvania. On this trip, he practiced "outdoor survival" techniques (in February snow, no less).

When his career took him to California, Todd used that opportunity to become an avid hiker and rock climber. Our family made a brief but memorable stop in Yosemite National Park during the "Last Great Family Vacation," taken the summer before our daughter's wedding.

We enjoyed Yosemite so much that Todd accompanied us back there for three more trips. On those trips, we made hikes to 11,000, 12,000 and 14,000 feet. On the second trip, we camped overnight near May Lake, at about 10,000 feet.[9] Todd did the cooking with fold-up kitchen utensils on a large rock overlooking a gorge. He prepared quiche and cappuccino. Incidentally, that was the first time my wife had slept outside overnight, and yes, even though it was freezing cold (in July), she loved it!

There's something special about the Yosemite wilderness and mountains. They leave a lasting impression. It's essentially a religious experience.

"The Chicken Came First!"

The Factors That Enabled Look About Lodge

"You have to know the past to understand the present."
—*Carl Sagan*

To understand Look About Lodge (the egg), you need to know a little about the Cleveland Natural Science Club (the chicken). Look About Lodge was a dream that became a reality for Cleveland Natural Science Club members in the 1930s.

Succinctly, the Cleveland Natural Science Club grew out of the early 1920s. It was during that time that Professor Ellis Persing would meet with his Education College students outside the classroom to carry on discussions about and do field work in the natural sciences. Nineteen of these students formed The Cleveland Nature Club with Professor Persing on May 21, 1924.

With the exuberance of youth, they would have discussions of plant and wildlife species, their habitats, and their impact on the Cleveland Metroparks reservations. The discussions and meetings would be at the School of Education, or at local libraries, and at Epworth Church.

Then, as the students became alumni, they reconstituted the group in September of 1925 as The Cleveland Natural Science Club. The natural sciences are characterized as the sciences of observation rather than dissection and experimentation. Natural scientists gather knowledge by observing nature, including plants, animals, geologic formations, and celestial bodies.

Article II of The Club's Constitution states:

"The purpose of the Club shall be to study and to promote the study of the natural sciences; to cultivate an appreciation of the great out-of-doors; to promote conservation of our natural resources and the protection of wild plant and animal life."

The complementing motto of Cleveland Metroparks is, "Conservation, Education, and Recreation."

Article III of the Science Club's Constitution sets forth the quite simple membership requirement as:

"Members shall be persons over eighteen years of age who are genuinely interested in the natural sciences."

Between 1924 and 1931, the fledgling Cleveland Natural Science Club held meetings in what is known as the "University Circle" area on the east side of Cleveland, and at Ellis Persing's home in Shaker Heights.

The two universities at University Circle, Western Reserve University (founded in 1826) and Case Institute of Technology (founded in 1880), relocated there during 1882 and 1885, respectively, across Euclid Avenue from the Wade Park Lagoon.

Cleveland Art Museum

They form the southern border of the area, and are the reason it was named University Circle. The two institutions then combined to form Case Western Reserve University in 1967.

In 1919-1920, the Euclid Ave. and Epworth Memorial congregations merged, creating the Epworth-Euclid Methodist Church. Between 1926 and 1928, the congregation built a dynamic new church building overlooking Wade Park Lagoon from the west.

The building is a modern adaptation of Gothic themes. The exterior is ornamented with figures by New York sculptor Leo Friedlander. On the interior, the roof is supported by four great arches with a large rose window, arched lateral windows, and four small lancet windows in the tower.[10]

The area also was, and is, home to a variety of educational and cultural institutions,[11] most with national and international reputations for excellence. The Western Reserve Historical Society moved to the area in 1898 and then relocated to the adjoining Hay and Hanna houses on East Boulevard in 1938-1941.

The internationally known Cleveland Art Museum was built at the north end of the Wade Park Lagoon in 1916. On the east side of the Lagoon is Severance Hall, home to the world renowned Cleveland Orchestra. Severance Hall was completed in 1931, the same year that the University Hospitals Medical Center was finished across Euclid Avenue from Severance Hall.

The Garden Center of Greater Cleveland was located on the east side of the lagoon from the 1920s until the 1960s. A new and much larger facility was then constructed in the Circle over the Wade Park ravine, just northeast of the Cleveland Art Museum. It is now called the Cleveland Botanical Garden.

Case Western Reserve University

In the 1830s, Cleveland's first natural history collections were housed in a small wooden building on Public Square. Its two rooms were crowded with animal specimens, earning it the nickname "The Ark." A number of Clevelanders had a passion for the natural sciences, which lead to the founding of the Cleveland Natural History Museum in 1920.

After spending three decades in a historic mansion on Euclid Avenue, The Cleveland Museum of Natural History moved to University Circle in 1952. Today, it is located just northwest of the Cleveland Art Museum. The Natural History museum also enjoys a national and international reputation for excellence. It was in this area, rich with cultural institutions, that "The Cleveland Natural Science Club" was born and grew. In fact, the Science Club grew out of the area.

By 1931, the Cleveland Natural Science Club needed a clubhouse as a base for their studies. Field trips would be planned to Cleveland Metropark reservations,[12] particularly to South Chagrin and Bedford. Nature trails were created by Science Club members in both these reservations. Field trips were nice, but the preference was to meet and work in close proximity to nature. They wanted to be surrounded by nature while providing natural science knowledge to the general public.

There was an old farmhouse in Bentleyville on Cleveland's east side. It was at the corner of River and Solon Roads on land that had been acquired by Cleveland Metroparks as part of the South Chagrin Reservation. Ellis Persing approached Cleveland Metroparks commissioners and asked for use of the farmhouse if the Club would fix up the building, maintain a nature trail, and provide nature education to the public. A bargain was struck, and the suburban Science Club was under way. The Science Club adopted the building as its clubhouse and named it Look-About-Lodge.

Severance Hall; Home to the World Famous Cleveland Orchestra

A Dedication to Nature and Public Education

The Cleveland Natural Science Club has always been dedicated to education because the founding members were teachers. Their first love and priority was to do research and further educate themselves in the natural sciences. However, the ultimate purpose was always to pass this knowledge on to others.

Throughout the Club's history, the focus has been on learning and teaching about wild plants and animals, plus preserving natural resources. The goal was always to "spread the word," giving more people knowledge about and an appreciation of the natural world.

The challenge was to attract members with the energy and imagination to provide programs and activities in support of the Cleveland Metroparks. All Science Club members were encouraged (and expected) to be active on one or more Club committees or sections.

On April 7, 1926, the club made its first field trip to Youngstown, Ohio. This began a series of field trips around Ohio and beyond for the purpose of expanding their knowledge of the natural sciences. Two years later, they held their first annual dinner on February 7, 1928.

Once they had a Look About Lodge, many of the Club's activities centered around their "clubhouse," but their activities always went beyond just functions at the Lodge.

The first full year of the Great Depression was 1930.[13] During this period in our nation's history, many people lost their jobs, then their homes, and, in some cases, took their own lives. It was truly, "the worst of times." Yet, a group of nature lovers was at work to make it, "the best of times."

Despite the hard economic times—or maybe partially because of them—membership in The Cleveland Natural Science Club grew. By 1935, the Club had grown to over two hundred members and had outgrown the farmhouse turned clubhouse.

Thus, in the middle of the Great Depression, Ellis Persing and the Cleveland Natural Science Club Trustees began planning for a new Look About Lodge!

Ironically, today's Look About Lodge was enabled in part by the Great Depression. Planning began in 1935 with construction starting in 1936. The Lodge building was completed in 1938, dedicated on June 5th, and opened to the public on June 23rd of that year.

Undoubtedly, some divine intervention caused the juxtaposition of occurrences that lead to the magnificent building you can visit and admire today. These include:

- The Early Naturalists Audubon, Burroughs, Muir, Seton, and Theodore Roosevelt who avidly promoted nature appreciation and conservation. It was their efforts that fostered the *back to nature* movement that arose in the early 1900s. It was their activity that resulted in America's National Park System and, in all probability, inspired the creation of Cleveland Metroparks and undoubtedly influenced college student interest in teaching the natural sciences.
- The Cleveland Metroparks grew out of the nature appreciation and conservation movement. The idea of William Stinchcomb, the emerald necklace (as the Park District is

known) encircles Cleveland on three sides. It was the Park District's directors that gave the Cleveland Natural Science Club its first clubhouse, and then enabled today's Look About Lodge to be built.

- The American Chestnut Blight that began killing these magnificent trees in the late 1800s, making them available for construction of the Lodge that we admire today.

- Cleveland Natural Science Club Founders and Members who were dedicated to serving the public before, during, and after their tenure in the old farmhouse, and who planned and financed today's Look About Lodge.

- Skilled Craftsmen from Greater Cleveland who built today's Look About Lodge when they were made available through the WPA[14] Program of the 1930s.

Look About Lodge
—A Sanctuary in the Woods

"I go to nature to be soothed and healed, and to have my senses put in order."

—*John Burroughs*

Although created as "clubhouses" for the Cleveland Natural Science Club, the Look About Lodges were much more than that. They were a sanctuary, a place to get away. It was like Henry David Thoreau's Walden Pond or John Burroughs' Slabsides.

The original Lodge began as, and today's still is, a "base camp" from which to study and better understand nature through both observation and inspiration. In addition, they were a place to get away from the stresses of daily life in the city. They were a sanctuary where members and visitors could be close to and commune with nature.

In the early years, the Lodges also served as a recreational and entertainment retreat. During the Great Depression, and throughout the years of World War II—before the days of television and computers—Look About Lodge was a venue for dancing, dinner parties, and cultural events such as plays and musical programs.

As described in the following pages, from its completion in 1938 until today, this extraordinary new Look About Lodge has given its occupants, and Greater Clevelanders, a focus. The Lodge offers a close-to-nature facility that enables educators to expand their own nature studies while providing both a natural location and rustic inspiration to Lodge visitors, including the public.

Throughout its history, especially, the new Lodge has embodied the dream of its creators: an inspiring place in which to acquire a deeper appreciation of nature and an understanding of the natural sciences.

Said to be one of the first nature education facilities in the country, it was, and is, truly a place to "go to nature to be soothed and healed and to have one's senses put in order." Look About Lodge was a larger version of Cleveland Metroparks other nature centers. North Chagrin had been built in 1931, the same year that the Cleveland Natural Science Club received use of the first Look About Lodge. Rocky River was completed in 1936, while the Brecksville stone cabin nature center, which was also built with WPA labor, was completed a year after the Lodge in 1939.

The Inauguration of Nature Appreciation that Enabled Cleveland Metroparks and Inspired Look About Lodge

"Heaven is under our feet as well as over our heads."
—*Henry David Thoreau*

For the first one hundred plus years of our country, most Americans lived very close to nature. They were colonists and farmers and plantation owners, or merchants serving these groups. Then, they were pioneers, ranchers, and miners.

Many of those individuals undoubtedly appreciated, and thanked God for, the beauties of the natural environment. However, most were essentially too busy *dealing* with nature to have the perspective needed to fully *appreciate* it. Possibly the best example of the transition from coping with nature to appreciating nature was the life of Ernest Thompson Seton. Seton went from wolf bounty hunter to conservationist. This transition made him one of America's most influential naturalists.

In Greater Cleveland, which is in Cuyahoga County, and in the counties of Lake, Geauga, Lorain, and Summit, essentially all children visit a park system during the course of their school studies. Many children also attend park system or Natural History Museum sponsored programs with their parents.

While this nature appreciation also occurs in other parts of our country, Greater Cleveland is fortunate to have an abundance of nature resources and nature-based organizations. In this part of the Western Reserve,[15] natural science organizations are essentially in stiff competition to provide residents a familiarity with the enjoyment of nature.

A little research reveals that our country has been blessed with many influential naturalists and wonderful parks.

To better understand the derivation of Look About Lodge, plus the Cleveland Natural Science Club and the Cleveland Metroparks, let's review some of the early naturalists who most influenced the phenomenal growth of America's interest in nature preservation and conservation.

There are, of course, a number of naturalists that could have been covered in this volume. This book wasn't intended to be a long tome, so only a half dozen of the most prominent naturalists are covered—and covered only briefly.

Without vociferous personalities such as Muir, Seton, and Roosevelt, we probably wouldn't have had a nature appreciation movement. In addition, we wouldn't have had a national park system that is unique in the world. It is what cinematographer Ken Burns calls, "America's Best Idea."

What America started, the world has followed. Today, there are over four hundred national parks in two hundred nations, and America's National Park System is still growing. It is interesting to note that under Interior Secretary Stewart Udahl, during the Kennedy and Johnson administrations, National Park set-asides had their greatest growth since Theodore Roosevelt.

As the History Channel points out, "You have to know the past to understand the present," so let's look at some of the men responsible for the inauguration of America's nature appreciation movement, which ultimately led to the creation of Look About Lodge.

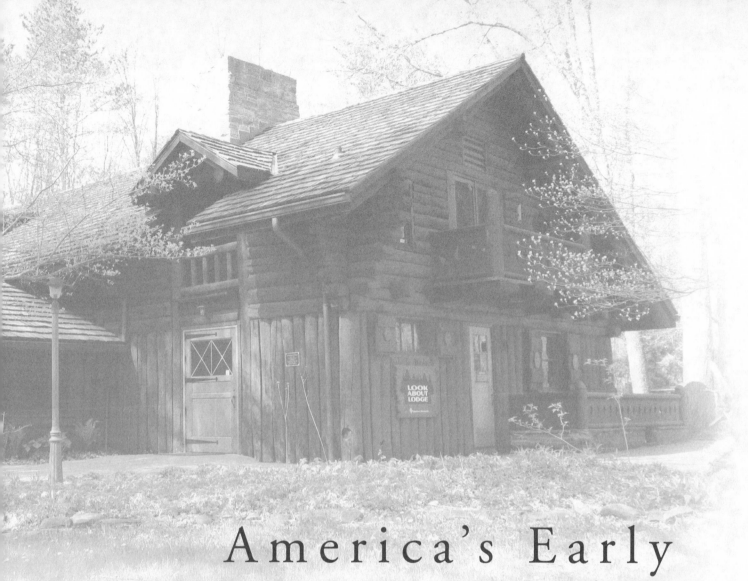

America's Early "Natural Scientists"

John Bartram
—Botanical Delineation

"What is a weed? A plant whose virtues have not yet been discovered."

—*Ralph Waldo Emerson*

John Bartram is described as the father of American botany. His botanical garden began as an eight-acre plot on the west bank of the Schuylkill River, about three miles above Philadelphia. Eventually, it grew to cover over 15 percent of the family's 102 acre farm.

Born on May 23, 1699, to a Quaker farm family, John Bartram's only formal education was from the local school. Most of his knowledge came from reading and observing. His birthday was some two hundred years after the Pilgrims' landing and seventy-seven years before America declared its independence.

Bartram was greatly interested in medicine and medicinal plants throughout his life. As an avid reader, he learned of Carolus Linnaeus, the Norseman responsible for creating the complex-compound Latin biological classification system we use today.[16] Bartram traveled widely throughout the colonies—from Lake Ontario to Florida, and "all the way west" to Ohio. He sent many of his botanical samples to Linnaeus for classification or verification.

Turning his collecting into a business, Bartram began distributing his plants to collectors throughout Europe. In 1765, his international reputation earned him the distinction of being named Royal Botanist by King George III of England.

Carolus Linnaeus called Bartram the "greatest natural botanist in the world." Bartram's plantings soon extended to sixteen acres, and were described as "the first true botanic collection in North America."[17] Bartram was also one of the co-founders, with Benjamin Franklin, of the American Philosophical Society in 1743.

John Bartram died September 22, 1777, in Philadelphia. John Bartrum's son, John Jr., acquired his father's interest in plants. In 1783, the younger Bartram compiled and published the first plant catalogue in America. It offered over four thousand species of native and exotic plants.

The Bartram plants were purchased by numerous Americans and by many Europeans. Some of the plants' notable destinations were Independence Hall in Philadelphia, George Washington's Mount Vernon, Thomas Jefferson's Monticello, and the E. I. DuPont Nemours estate.

William Bartram, the fifth of John and Ann Bartram's children, also followed in his father's footsteps. Well educated, William traveled the country to study flora, fauna, and Native American culture much as his father had done.

William then wrote a book on his experiences, calling it, "The Travels of William Bartram." This book is still in print in several editions.

As a child, Andrew Eastwick spent numerous enjoyable Sunday afternoons in Bartram's garden. As an adult, Eastwick made his fortune in the railroad business, and in 1850 purchased the Bartram garden stating, "It is my dearest hope that it be preserved forever." His purchase prevented the garden from being swallowed up by industrial sprawl.

Then, in 1891, Thomas Meehan, who had worked in the garden as a youth, became a Philadelphia City Councilman. He led a campaign to acquire the property as part of Philadelphia's public park system.

In 1893, years after John's death, descendants of John Bartram formed the John Bartram Association. This organization still operates the site as a museum in conjunction with Philadelphia's Fairmount Park Commission. It is billed as the Pre-revolutionary Home of John Bartram, a naturalist, botanist, and explorer.[18] Bertram was the first American to distinguish himself in the field of the natural sciences.

John Audubon
—Avian Documentation

"The richness I achieve comes from Nature, the source of my inspiration."

—*Claude Monet*

John James Audubon came to America from France in 1803 at the age of eighteen and became America's most prolific wildlife illustrator and bird naturalist. He created a collection of 435 life-sized prints, each accompanied with detailed notes about the species. The high quality of his paintings, along with his detailed written notes, were significantly better than other bird resources available at the time. This made Audubon the country's preeminent ornithologist.

Audubon's scientific knowledge, like Bartram's, was self-taught. His scientific methods included the first known banding of birds to reveal their migration patterns. He tied colored strings to the legs of Eastern Phoebes and discovered that the species returned to the same nesting sites each year.

John Audubon was probably born in Saint Dominguez—now Haiti—in 1785. (One source says he was born in New Orleans.) John Audubon's father was a French seafaring officer (another source says captain) and was also a plantation owner. John's mother was his father's mistress, so from the age of three, John was raised by his stepmother, Mrs. Audubon, in Nantes, France.

In 1803, his sea-going father sent eighteen-year-old John to America. The stated purpose was to supervise the family estate at Mill Grove, Pennsylvania, but the move was primarily made to avoid John's conscription into Emperor Napoleon's army.

The Audubon "estate" was some twenty miles west of Philadelphia on the Schuylkill River (about 17 miles further up the river from the property of John Bartram). While there, John Audubon hunted, studied, and developed an avid interest in birds and drawing. John Audubon was handsome, and quite popular with the ladies. "A handsomer man I never saw," one neighbor in Pennsylvania wrote. This attraction was partially due to his reputation for embellishing the tales he told. Audubon's "playing loose with the truth" may also be the reason for the uncertainty of his birthplace and other facts about his life.

It was during his brief two-year stay at Mill Grove that John met Lucy Bakewell. The Bakewells lived near the Audubon estate in Mill Grove. Mr. Bakewell admired Audubon for his well-trained dogs and marksmanship. As a well-educated girl, Lucy began to teach English to John, while John in turn gave Lucy some drawing skills.

Risking conscription, John Audubon returned to France in 1805 to ask his father's permission to marry. He also needed to discuss the family business plans. While in France, he met naturalist and physician Charles-Marie D'Orbigny. D'Orbigny improved Audubon's taxidermy skills and taught him scientific research methods.

When John returned to America, he resumed his bird studies and created his own personal nature museum. This was no doubt inspired by Philadelphia's magnificent Museum of Natural History. The Philadelphia Museum's bird exhibits were considered scientifically advanced at the time. Audubon's room in his home was packed with birds' eggs, stuffed raccoons, opossums, fish, snakes, and other creatures. He had become proficient at specimen preparation and taxidermy.

With his father's approval, John sold part of the Mill Grove farm, including the house. However, he did retain some of the land as an investment. He then went to New York to learn the import-export trade, hoping to find a way to support his marriage to Lucy. (Although he liked John, Mr. Bakewell wanted to see a reliable career from him before allowing his daughter to marry.) John married Lucy Bakewell in 1808.

John Audubon spent more than a decade in the dry goods business, endeavoring to support his interest in birding. During this period, he traveled down the Ohio River to Western Kentucky, setting up a general store in the still wild frontier town of Henderson on the Ohio River, some thirty miles east of the Indiana/Illinois border. John and Lucy moved into an abandoned log cabin. While there, Lucy gave birth to two sons, plus a daughter who died in infancy.

Like most of our country's other early naturalists, John Audubon lived a somewhat rugged life.[19] In the fields and forests, he wore typical frontier clothes and moccasins. Along with his musket he carried a ball pouch and a buffalo horn filled with gunpowder. On his belt were a butcher knife and a tomahawk. He continued to draw birds as a hobby, developing an impressive portfolio.

While he was successful in business for a while, eventually John fell on hard times. In 1819, he was briefly jailed for bankruptcy. He frequently turned to hunting and fishing to feed his family when business was slow.

Floating down the Mississippi, he lived a hand-to-mouth existence in the South while Lucy earned money as a tutor to well-to-do plantation families. On prospecting trips down river with a load of dry goods, John Audubon would join with Shawnee and Osage hunting parties. He picked up much of their wildlife knowledge, and then drew specimens and recorded scientific notes by the bonfire.

Audubon had great respect for Native Americans, and developed a deep appreciation for conservation. In his later writings, he warned about the destruction of birds and their habitats.

He spent a short period in Cincinnati, working as a naturalist and taxidermist at a museum. Audubon then took his gun, paint box, and taxidermy assistant Joseph Mason, and traveled down the Mississippi again. He had made a personal commitment to find and paint all the birds of North America for eventual publication.

From Kentucky, John and Lucy Audubon moved to Louisiana and then back north to Ohio. During a visit to Philadelphia in 1812, the year Congress declared war with Great Britain, Audubon renounced his French citizenship and become an American citizen.

John Audubon traveled everywhere from Labrador to Florida, and from Texas to the mouth of the Yellowstone River.[20]

It was said that John Audubon burned his earlier works in an effort to stimulate self-improvement. Another story is that on his return to Kentucky, he found that rats had eaten his entire collection of over two hundred drawings. Still a third story was that the art was ruined by gunpowder. Whatever the reason for the loss, it put him into weeks of depression. Audubon then took to the field again, determined to re-do his drawings to an even higher standard.

Eventually, John and Lucy decided to publish a life-size book of John's paintings, to be called *The Birds of America*. In 1826 Audubon sailed with his partly finished collection to England. This monumental work consisted of 435 hand-colored, life-size prints of 497 bird species.

Most people today know Audubon for his aviary contributions. In addition to his skills in painting and documenting, John Audubon discovered twenty-five new species of birds and twelve new subspecies. This was (and is) considered to be quite a feat for one person.

John Audubon also sold copies of the drawings to make extra money and to publicize his book. He had his portrait painted clothed as a frontiersman. The portrait was hung at the entrance of his exhibitions, promoting his rustic image.

His highly dramatic bird portraits, along with his embellished descriptions of wilderness life, were a big hit in Europe. The pages were organized for artistic effect and contrasting interest, as if the reader were taking a visual tour.

While in Edinburgh, Scotland, to seek subscriptions for the book, Audubon gave a demonstration of his method of propping up birds with wire at Professor Robert Jameson's Wernerian Natural History Association. As an interesting note, one of the students in the audience was Charles Darwin.

Audubon found a printer for the *Birds of America*, first in Edinburgh, then in London. He later collaborated with the Scottish ornithologist William MacGillivray on the *Ornithological Biographies*—life histories of each of the species in the work.

In 1845, Audubon published *First Imperial Folio*, a volume of the Viviparous Quadrupeds[21] of North America. Three years later, he suffered a stroke. After losing his eyesight, his son John Woodhouse Audubon completed work on his father's quadrupeds project.

It was on January 27, 1851 that the well-traveled and now somewhat famous John Audubon died.

John Audubon had no part in establishing the international society that carries his name, and which has made his name world famous. There was an indirect connection however. George Bird Grinnell was one of the founders of the Audubon Society in the late 1800s. Grinnell had been tutored by Lucy Audubon while growing up in Kentucky. Based on John Audubon's reputation for quality art and documentation, plus a dedication to conservation, George Grinnell chose the Audubon name for the organization. Part of the Society's mission was, and is, the protection of birds and their habitats.

Today, there is still an Audubon Center and sanctuary in Mill Grove, Pennsylvania. Containing 175 acres, including land from the original Audubon estate, it is a sanctuary for birds and other wildlife. This Center and sanctuary is one of many throughout the world dedicated to preserving the legacy of John James Audubon, while protecting birds and wildlife in their natural habitats. The sanctuaries are one more benefit that came out of the nature preservation movement.

John Burroughs
—Homespun Inspiration

"In all things of nature there is something of the marvelous. Nature does nothing uselessly."

—*Aristotle*

A highly popular nature writer of his time, John Burroughs was a prolific author of short stories and books, plus some twenty-three volumes of essays about nature. Known as the Hudson River naturalist, one reason for his popularity was a writing style which described nature in homespun "Ben Franklin" type terms. He has been called father of the American nature essay.[22]

John Burroughs was born on the family farm in the Catskill Mountains, near Roxbury, New York on April 3, 1837. His father and grandfather were staunch Baptists. As a schoolboy in the 1840s, Burroughs showed no interest in writing. Yet, in an 1857 letter to his bride Ursula, Burroughs apologized for his compulsive focus on nature and his determination to be an author.

One of his feats was writing *Notes on Walt Whitman as a Poet and Person*. Written in 1867, this was first biography published on Whitman.

John Burroughs succeeded in getting his articles published in at least three periodicals: *The Bloomville Mirror, Saturday Press*, and the *New York Leader*. Much of what he wrote appeared under the pseudonyms "Philomel" and "All Souls," along with titles like *Vagaries viz. Spiritualism, Fragments from the Table of an Intellectual Epicure*, and *Some of the Ways of Power*.

A Thought on Culture, was the first article published under his own signature, and it revealed his strong interest in nature. It includes extracts from some of his essays. The extracts show how, gradually but very definitely, nature edged into his essays and ultimately became the dominant theme.

About ten years after the letter to his bride, Burroughs issued his first book. When it was published, John had been working as a government employee in Washington, DC, for four years. Meanwhile, he was practicing his craft at every opportunity, polishing his skills and finding his niche.

In 1871, four years after the appearance of *Notes, Wake-Robin* was published. It was the first book in which the familiar Burroughs, the writer of essays on Nature, was revealed. It was the first in what eventually became a set of twenty-three volumes of collected essays, the last three of which were published posthumously.

One of John Burroughs' annoyances was writers that took liberty with the truth when describing wild animals. He wrote a piece for the *Atlantic Monthly* in 1903 titled, *Real and Sham Natural History* in which he deplored this twisting of natural truths.[23] John Burroughs denounced the new genre of writing as "yellow journalism of the woods." Burroughs suggested Seton's book *Wild Animals I Have Known* should have been titled *Wild Animals I* Alone *Have Known*.

The subject matter of Burroughs' twenty-three volumes was not limited to nature, although that was the dominant theme. His works also included philosophy, literary criticism, and travel. Burroughs' also made attempts at poetry. His poem *Waiting* offers insight into the influence that authors of the time such as Samuel Johnson and Ralph Waldo Emerson had on Burroughs.

The only reference to the Burroughs quote engraved into the assembly room of Look About Lodge was a notation that this also appeared at an inn in Michigan. However, you can see this quote very much fit Slabsides.

On his rustic house in the woods, he wrote, "…I was offered a tract of wild land, barely a mile from home, that contained a secluded nook and a few acres of level, fertile land shut off from the vain and noisy world by a wooded precipitous mountain…and built me a rustic house there, which I call 'Slabsides,' because its outer walls are covered with slabs. I might have given it a prettier name, but not one more fit, or more in keeping with the mood that brought me thither…Life has a different flavor here. It is reduced to simpler terms; its complex equations all disappear." From 1873, and for the rest of Burroughs' life, this area supplied much of the nature lore and inspiration which the naturalist recorded in his essays.

Slabsides still stands today. It is a rustic cabin, built in 1895 about one and a half miles from Burroughs' home on the Hudson. Burroughs used Slabsides for the last twenty years of his life. It was a place where he could write, study nature, and entertain his friends.

Due to Burroughs' fame, Slabsides became a mecca for nature lovers and writers. The guest books contain the names of hundreds of Burroughs admirers from the years 1897 to 1921. The visitors included Theodore Roosevelt, John Muir, Thomas Edison, and Henry Ford. Hundreds of visitors still come there each year.

In the early 1960s, Slabsides was threatened by local lumber interests. Funds were quickly raised, and today it sits on a 170-acre preserve. Designated a National Historic Landmark in 1968, it is preserved much as it was in Burrough's time.

It is essentially the same, both inside and out. Slabs of lumber, covered with bark, make up the exterior walls. The rustic red cedar posts that Burroughs set in place still hold up the porch. Inside, the furniture which Burroughs used, much of which he made, remains as it was.

Burrows died on March 29, 1921, near Kingsville, Ohio, while riding a train back from California. He was buried on his farm on his eighty-fourth birthday, April 3, 1921.

As a highly popular writer about nature, Burroughs readers were attracted to the way of life he wrote about and came to epitomize, "tantalizingly elusive yet universally accessible," simple values, simple means, and simple ends."[24]

John Muir
—Passionate Initiation

"Climb the mountains and get their good tidings.
Nature's peace will flow into you as sunshine flows into trees.
The winds will blow their own freshness into you…
while cares will drop off like autumn leaves."

–John Muir

Known as the prince of mountain lovers, John Muir was an early advocate of preserving this country's wilderness. His writings describe harrowing adventures, many of which were in the Yosemite area of the Sierra Nevada Mountains in California.

Muir was quoted as saying, "I live only to entice others to look at nature's loveliness." His activism was key to saving the Yosemite Valley, Sequoia National Park, Kings Canyon, and other wilderness areas.

The Sierra Club, which he co-founded in 1892, is now the largest and one of the most vocal nature preservation and environmental protection groups in the United States. True to his purpose in life, Muir's writings and philosophy, plus his Sierra Club, have strongly influenced the environmental movement in the United States, and around the world.

John Muir was born in Dunbar, Scotland, on April 21, 1838. Dunbar is on the coast of the North Sea. As a young boy John loved to climb around the remains of old Dunbar Castle.

When John Muir was seven years old, he entered Dunbar Grammar School. In addition to studying Latin, French, English, he learned mathematics and geography. When he read about natural history in a school reader, he was especially fascinated by America's fauna as described by John Audubon. He then spent considerable time wandering the local coastline and countryside.

At the age of eleven, his family left Scotland for the US settling in the milder climate of Wisconsin (about 10° in Latitude below his home in Scotland).

When he was twenty-two, Muir enrolled in the University of Wisconsin, despite having had little schooling since the age of eleven. He stayed in college only two and a half years, studying primarily the natural sciences.

After college, young John worked as a mechanic in a carriage shop. He spent most of the Civil War in Canada. Then, in 1867, he had a life-changing experience. While working in the carriage shop, a file he was working with slipped and went into his eye. He then quickly lost sight in the other eye. "This was the darkest period of his life." As his sight slowly returned, John Muir felt "reborn." From then on, he dedicated his life to seeing "America's natural wonders," which he had almost been deprived of viewing.

Saying that he couldn't get enough of wild beauty, he set out to walk the thousand miles from Louisville, Kentucky, to Savannah, Georgia. He had hoped to travel to the headwaters of the Amazon and work his way to the sea, but he contracted malaria.

In March of 1868 at the age of thirty, he ended up in San Francisco. When he inquired to learn the nearest way out of town, Muir was asked where he wanted to go. He replied, "To any place that is wild." This led him to Yosemite.

In Yosemite, Muir worked as a shepherd and then ran a sawmill near the base of Yosemite Falls. He continued to study nature saying that, "Nature was written in capitals in the awesome stones of the Sierra Nevada."

John Muir served as a guide for many of Yosemite's prominent visitors. This included one of his idols, Ralph Waldo Emerson. In 1903, he gave a tour to President Theodore Roosevelt.

Muir's lust for travel took him to Alaska several times. It was said, "He braved Alaskan storms with only a crust of bread in his pocket." (Remember, Muir's birthplace overlooked the North Sea, so he was used to harsh, cold weather.)

Eventually John Muir left Yosemite, at first for just a few months at a time. Then, in 1880, he became an orchard grower and married Wanda Strentzel. They lived near Martinez, a town on an inlet of the San Francisco Bay, just north of Oakland. John Muir still traveled to Yosemite periodically, becoming convinced that, unless something was done, the glorious wilderness he had found in 1868 would soon disappear into private use and development.

In the 1880s, *Century* was one of the most prominent magazines in the country. In 1889 Muir took the magazine's editor, Robert Underwood Johnson, on a camping trip to Tuolumne Meadows. Tuolumne is in the high Sierras at about eight thousand feet, some two thousand feet above the Yosemite Valley.

Muir wrote a collection of articles for *Century Magazine*, entitled "Studies in the Sierra." The series promoted National Park status for Yosemite. Muir and Underwood actively lobbied the US Congress to make Yosemite a National Park. Both men were interested in saving Yosemite from private development. Each sought to inspire the other to help prevent the subalpine environment of the High Sierra from being destroyed by sheep farming. Yosemite was first set aside as a park by the State of California in 1864. Yosemite became a National Park in 1890, along with Sequoia and Kings Canyon. These were the second, third, and fourth wilderness areas to become national parks.

In 1892, John Muir wrote to Robert Underwood Johnson, again saying, "Let us do something to make the mountains glad." That was the year Johnson joined with Muir to form the Sierra Club. The Yosemite Valley was then being managed by the state of California. The Sierra Club's purpose was to preserve more of the Sierra Nevada and make it available to the public. The little book he began in 1900 would remain in print throughout the twentieth century, inspiring generations of Americans with his love of the natural world.[25]

By the early 1900s, the growing City of San Francisco was in need of water, so there was a push to build a dam across the Grand Canyon of the Tuolumne River at the mouth of

Hetch Hetchy[26] Valley. This valley, which was comparable in size and beauty to the Yosemite Valley, lay to the north of Tuolumne Meadows.

The battle for preservation over development was presented and argued on the front pages and editorial pages of the nation's newspapers. Muir summed up the basic arguments against the dam in some of his most profound words, "These temple destroyers, devotees of ravaging commercialism, seem to have a perfect contempt for nature. Instead of lifting their eyes to the God of the mountains, (they) lift them to the almighty dollar. Dam Hetch Hetchy! As well dam for water-tanks the people's cathedrals and churches, for no holier temple has ever been consecrated by the heart of man."

Ironically, Muir also wrote, "The love of nature among Californians is desperately moderate; consuming enthusiasm is almost wholly unknown." (What a difference a century makes.) Over seven decades later, in 1976, the California Historical Society voted John Muir "The Greatest Californian."

Muir lost the fight against damming Hetch Hetchy. It was said that the building of that dam and reservoir contributed to John Muir's death from pneumonia. California's great mountain man died on Christmas Eve of his seventy-sixth year, December 24, 1914. His many writings, as well as the co-founding of the Sierra Club, had a tremendous impact on preserving and protecting the wilderness and wildlife.

Ernest Thompson Seton —A True Transformation

"You must in some sort note it down and pass it on to another way seeker."

—*Ernest Thompson Seton*

Ernest Thompson Seton is acknowledged as one of America's most influential naturalists. A prolific writer and artist, Seton authored and illustrated some sixty books, plus probably more than one thousand magazine articles and short stories. In addition, he drew or painted some six thousand works of art.

Seton's writings differed from those of Burrows. Seton's were more from the perspective of a naturalist and student of nature. While they were both interesting and inspirational, like Muir, Seton was more factual than philosophical.

His book, *Wild Animals I Have Known*, has been continuously in print since its original edition in 1898. Ernest Thompson Seton is considered a founder of the American wildlife conservation movement. His teachings, writings, and illustrations have informed countless Americans, as well as nature lovers around the world, about natural history.

Seton is credited with being a leading early influence in the emergence and growth of the American conservation and nature appreciation movement. His subsequent contributions to the sciences of ecology, mammalogy, and animal behavior made him a pivotal figure in the English-speaking world.

Seton was also a strong advocate of the outdoors life through the Woodcraft League and the Boy Scouts, based on the promotion of Native American traditional values.

Born Ernest Thompson in the English town of Durham in 1860, Ernest took on a new last name after a disagreement with his father. The Seton name was also in his family lineage.

Durham is on England's northern border with Scotland, about one hundred miles south of John Muir's birthplace. Both of Ernest's parents were from Scotland.

The eighth of ten brothers, Ernest moved to eastern Canada with his family when he was six. While in the British Isles, Ernest's father had lost his fortune in the shipping industry. After trying farming (unsuccessfully) for four years in eastern Canada, his father became an accountant in Toronto.

During his early education in Toronto, Ernest met the son of a Dr. William Brodie, and the two boys studied natural history under Brodie's tutelage. As a youth, Ernest retreated to the woods to draw and study animals as a way of avoiding his abusive father.

Seton became interested in art in his early teens, and at the age of nineteen, he returned to England to pursue a scholarship from the Royal Academy of Art. After studying there for only two years (of his seven-year scholarship), Ernest's health was suffering due to bad food and deplorable living conditions. He returned to Canada and again studied the natural sciences under Dr. Brodie.

Two of Ernest's older brothers had homesteads in Manitoba, and Ernest joined them there in 1881 at the age of twenty-one. Although he tried farming, he was always distracted by his thirst for knowledge about the natural sciences.

He would go off into the sand hills for days and weeks on end; thus, he was considered lazy and odd by the conventional people of the town. However, he did subsequently become "Naturalist to the Government of Manitoba."

During his twenties, Seton did extensive animal research and drew animal art. He also wrote natural history articles, and exchanged skins for study with other naturalists in Canada and in the United States. This is how Seton first met Theodore Roosevelt.

While in Canada, Seton hunted wolves for the bounty. In fact, he combined his study of wolves with his bounty hunting experience and wrote a book called, "How to Catch Wolves."

In 1893, then in is thirties, Seton left Canada to take a job as wolf bounty hunter in New Mexico. He then settled in the United States for the remainder of his life.

This job was in the still-wild canyon area of northeast New Mexico. The local ranchers had retained Seton to kill a dangerous outlaw who had been attacking their livestock. That outlaw was a wolf named Lobo.

Based on his experiences and study Seton came to the New Mexico territory with poison, traps, and a rifle. He expected to stay but a few weeks to collect the unusually high one thousand dollar bounty for Lobo.

While he sought Lobo, Seton observed the diminishing herds of prong horned sheep, deer, elk, and buffalo. These herbivores had roamed the planes in large herds until the arrival of the white man.

The Native Americans and wolves had shared the herds, and all had thrived, but the settlers came in such large numbers, and killed so many deer, elk, and buffalo, that the balance shifted, and the herds were diminished. Ranchers then replaced the wild herds with cattle who, due to their breeding, were easy prey for the wolves.

The PBS documentary titled *The Wolf That Changed America*[27] revealed how Seton's efforts to kill Lobo transformed his perspective on the natural world. Lobo, an alpha wolf, had taken a mate, a white wolf the ranchers called Bianca.

Wolves are highly intelligent, with a pack of up to a dozen living as a family with the breeding pair—the alpha male and female. During breeding season, late winter through early spring, the alpha wolves are inseparable. Knowing this, Seton set a trap for Bianca. He was successful and killed Bianca. Lobo, in essence, lost his spirit when his mate was killed. Thus, Seton eventually tracked down Lobo, and killed him, but before he did, he and Lobo had a transforming eye-to-eye contact. This is what led to Seton's transformation.

After his Lobo showdown, Seton began asking *why*; why was so much wildlife in such poor condition? What was our relationship with nature, and why were we destroying it. Thus, Ernest Thompson Seton evolved from bounty hunter to a naturalist and conservationist.

In 1899, he published a book titled *Wild* Animals I Have Known. The book was an immediate success throughout the world, making Seton internationally famous and turning him into somewhat of a celebrity. His international reputation continued through much of the twentieth century,[28] and today, *Wild Animals I Have Known* is still in print in several editions.

While continuing to publish books and articles, Seton lobbied heavily for conservation. He used his notoriety to push for the first legislation that protected migratory birds and animals.

This was the impetus for continuing government set-asides of wilderness areas and the protection of interstate wildlife. It was the early 1900s, and Seton's efforts became the foundation of today's environmental movement.

Seton believed that it wasn't enough for people to be aware of nature; he believed that nature had to be experienced. This is why he founded the Woodcraft Indians—predecessor to The Boy Scouts of America.

Seton, like Muir, yearned to travel. In 1907, he returned to Northern Canada to take a two-thousand-mile, seven-month canoe trip, exploring the Hudson's Bay Company routes.

As a lifetime learner, Seton became an expert in Native American sign language while learning about wildlife from the American Indians' perspective.

In 1908, Seton moved to Greenwich, Connecticut. While there, in 1928, Seton was awarded the internationally prestigious "John Burroughs Medal" by the US National Institute of Sciences. This was in recognition of Seton's book, "Lives of Game Animals."

Then, in 1930 (at the age of seventy), Seton became a citizen of the United States. He lived his last years in the stone "castle" he designed and built in the 1930s. Located just outside of Santa Fe, New Mexico, he used the castle to house The Academy for the Love of Learning, which he had also founded. He invited leaders of recreational organizations and young people from around the country to attend the institute's programs. Seton's lifetime lesson was that nature should be respected and "well-tended," and should not be consumed and destroyed. The Cleveland Natural Science Club used this approach on a local basis to train scout and youth group leaders.

Today, Seton's art, books, and natural history collections are housed and maintained by two institutions. One is the Academy for the Love of Learning, which now occupies Seton's castle.

The Academy is located on eighty-six acres of the original two thousand five hundred acres owned and developed by Ernest Thompson Seton. The seven thousand square foot home had thirty rooms. Seton's unique castle is six miles southeast of Santa Fe.

The other repository for Seton's works is the Philmont Museum, owned and operated by the Boy Scouts of America. The Philmont Museum honors Seton's many contributions to scouting.

Philmont is also located in New Mexico outside of Cimarron, just east of the where Seton had his transforming encounter with Lobo the wolf. Philmont is about 150 miles northeast of Santa Fe and Seton's castle.

Ernest Thompson Seton died at his castle in northern New Mexico in 1946 at the age of eighty-six. He had spent a lifetime raising awareness of the impact that humans have on their environment. One of his missions was to introduce young people to view the natural world as an enduring source of learning and to inspire them with nature's wonders.

The Boy Scouts of America: Nature Appreciation for the Young at Heart

Ernest Thompson Seton co-founded the Boy Scouts of America and authored the first Boy Scout Handbook. Seton also held the title of *Chief Scout* from 1910 until 1915.

Today's scouting movement began in England by a fifty-year-old bachelor named General Robert Baden-Powell. One of the few heroes of Britain's Boer War, Baden-Powell's specialty was military scouting. He documented his ideas in a book for the military titled, "Aids to Scouting."

When General Baden-Powell's book became popular among young boys, he modified it to be applicable for youth. In 1907, General Baden-Powell tested the application of his ideas to youth at a camp for boys on Brownsea Island, located off England's southern coast about one hundred miles southwest of London.

The camping experience for boys proved highly successful. Baden-Powell then rewrote his military book, calling it simply, "Scouting for Boys." This book took ideas from a number of sources, including Seton's writings. The social climate was right for the youth program called "Scouting." It spread quickly around the British Commonwealth, then to other countries.

Meanwhile, in the United States in 1901 to 1902, Seton founded the Woodcraft Indians. The organization was based on the American Indian culture for which Seton had gained great respect. Seton's code of ethics for the Woodcraft Indians was adopted by the Boy Scouts, and has been internalized by generations of boys.

Seton had visited England in 1904, where he met with Baden-Powell and gave him a copy of his manual for the Woodcraft Indians. This is how Seton's ideas became part of the British Boy Scout program.

In 1910, Ernest Thompson Seton became chairman of the founding committee of the Boy Scouts of America.

The Boy Scouts of America got its sustaining organization structure from Chicago publisher William Boyce. In February of 1910, there were several other loosely structured, outdoor oriented youth organizations, some using the name "Boy Scout" and some using other names. Some were even using a variation of the British Scout program.

Boyce organized the Boy Scouts of America as a business. He incorporated the organization in Washington, DC, rather than in Chicago, and recruited key youth professionals to design and operate the program. Boyce then provided key funding for the effort.

The new Boy Scouts of America established a national office and developed a temporary handbook. In addition, the Boy Scouts of America sought and received Baden-Powell's endorsement. The US scout leaders then began working to get a Congressional Charter from the US Congress, which was finally obtained in 1916.

In the introduction of the original Boy Scout Handbook edition, Seton made it clear that he considered himself to be the real founder of the World Scouting movement, saying, "In 1904, I went to England to carry on the work of fostering a Woodcraft and Scouting movement there. Knowing General

Baden-Powell to be the chief advocate of scouting in the British Army, I invited him to cooperate with me, in making the movement popular."

Accordingly, in 1908 Seton organized his Boy Scout movement, incorporating the principles of the Woodcraft Indians with other ethical features such as savings banks, fire drills, etc. Baden-Powell gave it a partly military organization plus a carefully compiled and fascinating book.

When William Boyce incorporated the Boy Scouts of America, Seton merged his Woodcraft Indians with the new organization and became the BSA's first Chief Scout.

James West, a Washington, DC, attorney, active in juvenile cases, was recruited in 1911 as the BSA Executive Secretary. West soon changed his title to Chief Scout Executive. James West created a well-organized national structure that was a key to the organization's growth and reputation. Although he had intended to make Scouting only a temporary diversion from his legal career, West remained the Chief Scout Executive until his retirement in 1943.

Both West and Seton were strong-willed, so conflicts soon arose on how Scouting was to be developed. Seton considered West to be simply an administrator and challenged West's authority to control the young program's development. West had established the organization's power base and was able to force Seton out in 1915. West then removed all of Seton's writing from the Boy Scout Handbook by its fourteenth printing in 1916, but Seton had made his mark and is now remembered as a major contributor to the movement.

Seaton's key role in the Boy Scouts of America reveals his mission of getting young boys interested in nature appreciation (mentioned earlier). This, of course, leads to these boys being nature lovers in their adult years which is what happened with my father.

Theodore Roosevelt
—Dynamic Facilitation

"Parks are the country estates of the people."

—Theodore Roosevelt

On September 6, 1901, President William McKinley was shot while attending the Pan American Exposition in Buffalo, New York. At the time, Theodore Roosevelt, his Vice President, was on a hiking trip with his family at Mount Tahawus in the Adirondacks.

TR was summoned to Buffalo, and on September 14, 1901, Theodore Roosevelt became the twenty-sixth President of the United States at the age of forty-two. Roosevelt was the youngest man ever to become President.

TR has been called "the accidental President" [29] because when he was selected to be Vice President; it was never expected that he would become President. Yet, Roosevelt has consistently been ranked by scholars as one of the greatest US Presidents.

Theodore was called "Teedie," by his family, although it was said he hated the nickname.

In the early 1880s, Roosevelt had established two cattle ranches in what was then the Dakota Territory (now part of North Dakota). Thus, he was familiar with the wide-open spaces, plus the natural fauna and flora. This may have been a contributing factor to Roosevelt's unfettered enthusiasm for nature. He became a strong champion of wilderness protection, which led to many initiatives on conservation and nature preservation during his presidency. Roosevelt's focus on nature included the creation of four additional National Parks and the set-aside of 230 million acres of wilderness under the Antiquities Act.

A loving father of six children, Roosevelt thought much about the future and what the children of that time would inherit. This is another reason he was so influenced by naturalists such as John Muir, Ernest Thompson Seton, and others. TR became widely recognized as a naturalist [30] and as a president who adamantly supported America's conservation and nature preservation movement.

In 1903, Roosevelt was shown Yosemite by John Muir, who was also a strong advocate of nature conservation. With the urgings of Seton and Muir, Roosevelt established the Antiquities Act in 1906, shepherding it through Congress. This act was officially defined as, *An Act for the Preservation of American Antiquities* (16 USC 431-433). This act allowed a president to set aside by executive order national landmarks, historic sites, and other lands, protecting them from development, presumably until the Congress designated them as National Parks or some other national set-aside. The purpose of this Act was to protect a variety of prehistoric Indian ruins and artifacts. The legislation allowed land to be protected much more quickly than by going though the Congress to create a National Park.

Although this act was intended for small historic sites, it was first used to protect a large area designated as Devils Tower National Monument by Roosevelt in 1906. The Act has been used over a hundred times since its enactment. In fact, only three presidents have not used the act to set aside parkland: Presidents Nixon, Reagan, and George H. W. Bush.

The Grand Canyon's 230 million acres was first given Federal protection in 1893 as a *forest reserve*, and then later as a National Monument. The Canyon did not become a National Park until 1919, some three years after the National Park Service was established.

Theodore Roosevelt's comment on the national parks concept is as follows:

> "It is the preservation of the scenery, the forests, and the wilderness game for the people as a whole, instead of leaving the enjoyment thereof to be confined to the very rich. It is noteworthy that in this essential democracy one of the best bits of national achievement which our people have to their credit; and our people should see to it that this is preserved for their children and their children's children forever with the majestic beauty unmarred."

Roosevelt believed that natural resources must be used for the benefit of all the people, not monopolized for the benefit of the few. Before there were national parks in the US, most parkland in Europe and elsewhere was owned by the rich and reserved for their use.

To TR, conservation meant development as much as it meant protection. He recognized the right and duty of his generation to develop and make the natural resources of our land accessible and not to waste them. Roosevelt considered it each generation's responsibility to preserve the land, including the wilderness, for those who would come after us.

Roosevelt signed the Antiquities Act into law on June 8, 1906. This enabled "historic landmarks, historic and prehistoric structures, and other objects of historic or scientific interest to be classified as national monuments…the limits of which in all cases shall be confined to the smallest area compatible with the proper care and management of the objects to be protected." This enabled restricting the use of government owned land without Congressional oversight. As might be expected, this often causes a controversy within Congress.

TR was also a writer. In 1893, he authored *The Wilderness Hunter*. Then in 1897, his *American Ideals* was published. An ardent speech giver, in October of 1898, he opened the campaign for president with a speech titled *The Duties of a Great Nation*.

One of TR's pet peeves was "nature fakers"—writers who took liberties with *mother nature's children*.[31] Fables were all right if they were labeled as fables or folk tales, but when exaggerated claims were made of animals acting in humanistic ways, TR did not appreciate it. Roosevelt praised Ernest Thompson Seton for his "interesting observations of fact," but cautioned Seton on mingling imagination with truth. TR was a close friend and naturalist colleague of John Burroughs, who also decried what he called "yellow journalism of the woods."

Edward B. Clark, the Washington correspondent for the Chicago Evening Post, had a fireside chat with Roosevelt on the subject of nature. With Roosevelt's approval, he then published an article describing Roosevelt's negative feelings about the practice. The main concern of the true naturalists was that this misinformation was being taught in schools as fact. Clark attributed the term "nature fakers" to Roosevelt, and it immediately became a colloquialism.

Roosevelt's qualifications to judge the writings on American wildlife were justified by Dr. C. Hart Merriam, chief of the US Biological Survey. Merriam referred to the many valuable specimens Roosevelt had brought back from his hunting expeditions, and stated that they had contributed greatly to factual zoological knowledge.

Such were the lives of six naturalists who each were instrumental in the nature preservation movement. So how did the nature conservation movement evolve, and become the inspiration for Look About Lodge?

Parkland For All
The People

National Preservation

In 1870, the Washburn-Langford-Doane Expedition[32] was formed to explore the stories of incredible natural wonders in the Yellowstone area. The expedition was started by three men: Cornelius Hedges, Nathaniel P. Langford, and William H. Clagett. The expedition was financed by its members.

Hedges, born in Montana Territory in October of 1831, had earned three degrees—two from Yale and a law degree from Harvard. He began his twenty-year newspaper career with the Helena Daily Herald in 1865.

Henry D. Washburn was a lawyer who practiced in Newport, Indiana, and later became a politician there. Born in Windsor, Vermont, on March 28, 1832, he had also been a lieutenant colonel in the Union Army.

Nathaniel P. Langford was born in St. Paul, Minnesota, in 1832. He was an explorer, businessman, historian, and government official. Langford had played an important role in the early years of the Montana gold fields.

William H. Clagett was born in Upper Marlboro, Maryland, on September 21, 1838. He moved to Keokuk, Iowa, with his father in 1850, and subsequently became a lawyer and then a Montana Congressman in 1870.

Gustavus C. Doane was the Army Lieutenant that lead the expedition's Army escort.

The story that has been promulgated through the years is as follows:

"When the expedition's members began discussing how to divide the land into personal claims, Cornelius Hedges suggested that, rather than capitalize personally on their discoveries, that the members seek to have the land set aside for all time as a reserve for the use and enjoyment of all the people.

"After retiring from their campfire, some of the explorers later admitted that the prospect of establishing a national park was so exciting they couldn't sleep."

Thus goes the popular version of how the "National Park" idea was born.[33] From the perspective of time, the facts aren't as important as the reality of what came to be—the United States National Park System—which is unique in the world.

As Ken Burns[34] puts it, "It's like baseball, like jazz, it's an American invention."

Little did these early adventurers realize what would happen during the next one hundred plus years. Today, over twenty-one million acres of land, lakes, and rivers have been turned into fifty-eight national parks, eighty national monuments, forty-five national historical parks, numerous national battlefields, and other historic preservation areas.

During the summer of 1871, the US Geological Survey did a follow-up investigation into the wonders described by the Washburn-Langford-Doane Expedition. Hedges, the well-educated newspaperman, Langford, the experienced bureaucrat, and Clagett, the lawyer and new Montana Congressman, then drew up national parks legislation. The National Park Act was presented to the US House of Representatives on December 18, 1871.

After gaining the endorsement by the House Committee on Public Lands and the Secretary of the Interior, the Parks Act was adopted by the House on January 30, 1872. It then passed by the Senate on February 27, receiving the signature of President Ulysses S. Grant on March 1, 1872. Thus was the amazing speed with which our government enabled Yellowstone to become our country's first national park.

Conservation Gets a Fresh Meaning

"It's not what you look at that matters, it's what you see."
—Henry David Thoreau

The National Parks Act of 1872 was the first time the US Government had preserved land for a new purpose. Previously, the term conservation had been applied to coal, iron ore, and other raw materials of industry. Conservation was now being applied to land removed from commercial use and set aside for public use.

In 1852, the US Congress had designated The Hot Springs Reservation in Arkansas as a national resource because of the medicinal qualities believed to be possessed by its waters, but the reservation didn't become a national park until 1921.

Yellowstone—the first national park—achieved national park status in 1872, and is the only multi-state national park. Primarily in Wyoming, Yellowstone also extends into Montana and Idaho.

We know now that much of Yellowstone is a volcanic crater whose eventual eruption will cause a catastrophe in the United States—and probably the world. But, let's let sleeping dogs lie and hope the eruption holds off for a few more centuries, or maybe a millennia.

The educational value of national parks is multi-dimensional. Numerous natural science aspects of each park are researched and documented in guidebooks. Information on both flora and fauna is provided, as well as on the park's geological history.

Knowledge learned—or relearned—in a recreational setting gives a new context to what a person may have been exposed to in a classroom or even have become familiar with in and around his or her hometown. For example, when growing up in the East or Midwest, you may have become familiar with the relatively common blue jay. Then, when visiting the west, you are exposed to the stellar jay of the same bird genus but a different species.

In the classroom, you learned of the ice age, but upon visiting Yellowstone or Yosemite, you become aware of how much of our continent was affected by the ice age. As a park visitor, you learn that rocks and boulders strewn about by the ice age are called erratics and have been there for thousands of years. (There are even some erratics in New York City's Central Park.)

In addition, you may have been taught that glaciers caused depressions in the land as they did when forming the Great Lakes, and you learned that water flowing through what began as a depression can create deep gorges. Then, you see momentous natural wonders such as the Grand Canyon of the Yellowstone or Grand Canyon National Park in Arizona, and your earlier education "comes to life."

Also, it is interesting to note that national parks are still being created, and that our appreciation for nature is continually evolving. The Cuyahoga Valley National Park just south of Cleveland, Ohio, was established in 1974, while five national parks in Alaska, one in South Carolina, and another in American Samoa have been established since then.[35]

As an interesting aside, the Cuyahoga Valley National Park is one of the most visited of the national parks. The reason for this is that the Cuyahoga Valley National Park is essentially surrounded by metropolises. It is within a short driving distance of many people. To visit most national parks. people have to make a planned trip many miles from their homes. This usually requires an overnight stay, so the Cuyahoga Valley National Park functions much as a metro-park.

Preservation Is About Resurgence

"The sun, moon and stars would have disappeared long ago…
had they been within reach of predatory human hands."
—*Henry Ellis*

With conservation, land is protected from human intervention and allowed to reestablish the plants and trees that are natural to the area. The reestablishment of animal life follows, but the overall natural balance takes a little longer. Our country's early European settlers invested much time and effort in altering nature's balance. They diligently cleared wilderness land for human habitation and crop propagation. For several hundred years, they killed wildlife in great numbers, including wolves. The wolves were killed to prevent them from feeding on domestic cattle and sheep, which were easier prey than most wildlife.

The recklessness of wolf killing by humans is now known. The natural balance lesson is best exemplified by the return of wolves to our first national park—Yellowstone. Wolves are at the top of nature's food chain, a position they share with bears. Wolves kill and eat deer and elk, as well as other mammals all the way down the chain to moles and mice.

In Yellowstone, with the wolves gone, the deer and elk multiplied. Without wolf competition, coyotes multiplied. This diminished the smaller rodent population that coyotes feed on, such as squirrels and moles. As smaller rodents became scarce, other smaller predators like foxes and badgers were also diminished. The Coyotes also fed on pronghorn sheep calves, thus greatly reducing this species.

The increased deer and elk herds of Yellowstone began feeding on more of the tender young shoots and mature tree bark of aspen and cottonwood trees, as well as willow shrubs. After a 1988 forest fire in Yellowstone reduced the maturing trees and shrubs, the new shoots of this flora were eaten by the deer and elk, preventing replenishment of the forest. This reduced the beaver population that had used this plant life for food and housing. It also reduced the songbirds that had used it for nesting and as a migratory way station.

Wolves were returned to the Yellowstone area in 1995 and 1996 from the human intervention of trapping wolves in Canada and releasing them in Yellowstone. The elk herds were soon reduced by becoming a food source, and the coyotes were reduced due to wolf competition. Amazingly, within a decade, the trees and shrubs, plus the beaver, badgers, and birds, began returning. We are fortunate to have had many naturalists and authors whose insights enabled this resurgence, and who have documented the effect of wolves on nature's balance.[36]

In 1935, the Wilderness Society was founded to combat "the ever-expanding highway system in the US" The Society began publishing a magazine that called attention to "the emergency in conservation which requires no delay in curtailing the craze to build highways everywhere."

Or, as Charles Kuralt put it, "Thanks to the Interstate Highway System, (which, of course, came much later), it is now possible to travel from coast to coast without seeing anything."

The Refocus to Environmental Protection

"Conservation is about cultivating a partnership with nature, rather than a dictatorship over nature."
—*Barbara Holtz, CIP,*
Naturalist Manager, Look About Lodge

While John Bartram's history doesn't mention a concern with nature preservation, Audubon, Burroughs, Muir, Seton, and Theodore Roosevelt were definitely committed to saving the wilderness, including the protection and continued existence of native wild species.

As stated previously, the main concern was the diminishing wild bird and animal populations. There was also a stated concern about the preservation of forests as habitats. One objective was to enable Americans and other visitors to experience the atmosphere of forests and woodlands.

The National Parks Act of 1872 recognized the need for wilderness set-asides. The emphasis of conservation protection in the 1800s and the early 1900s was on the preservation of wilderness areas.

The environmental movement began in the mid twentieth century. "Environmentalists advocate the sustainable management of resources and stewardship of the environment."[37] Environmentalism focuses more on conserving the air we breathe, the water we drink, and the food we eat—with nature preservation taking a back seat. Then the atomic age brought the harmful effects of radiation, which ushered in a whole new set of environmental challenges.

One early environmental incident occurred in October of 1948. A temperature inversion over the Western Pennsylvania town of Donora trapped atmospheric pollutants from the Zinc Works of the US Steel Corporation for six days. The pollution extended over eastern Ohio, plus parts of Maryland and West Virginia. This incident caused more than five thousand people to become ill from the polluted air.

Then, in 1950, a Japanese fishing vessel was exposed to deadly radiation from a hydrogen bomb test blast. These incidents, and others less drastic, stimulated the concern over atmospheric pollution and contamination that was introduced with the August 1945 bombings of Hiroshima and Nagasaki.

In 1962, Rachel Carson published *Silent Spring*, alerting the general public to the dangers of pesticides. Carson summarized her main argument as, "The 'control of nature' is a phrase conceived in arrogance, born of the Neanderthal age…when it was supposed that nature exists for the convenience of man."

These factors, and others, helped the country's interest in conservation morph into the environmental movement. We began focusing more on the air, water, food, and fuel we need to survive. Thus, the term conservation had come full circle, from conserving our natural, raw materials such as coal and iron ore to protecting nature and its surroundings, and now back to protecting resources and the environment in which we live. Fortunately, our interest in wilderness and wildlife remains, but it is sharing the stage with ecology and the finite resources of energy.

In 1955, the first Air Pollution Control Act was passed by the US Congress after a number of states had passed such legislation. The national act recognized the seriousness of air pollution and established a national standard. It also granted five million dollars annually for five years for research by the Public Health Service.

This funding was extended in 1960, and, in 1962, amendments enforced the principle provisions of the original act. They also called for research to be done by the US Surgeon General to determine the health effects of various motor vehicle exhaust substances.

Also by the 1960s, the debilitating effects of radiation from atom bomb tests was becoming better known. Shortly thereafter, concern about pesticides and other environmental contamination began to be publicized.

In 1963, Congress passed "An act to improve, strengthen, and accelerate programs for the prevention and abatement of air pollution." This legislation was updated in 1970 and again in 1990.

In 1969, a small fire was ignited in oil and debris on Cleveland's Cuyahoga River, causing little or no damage. The fire was out within thirty minutes. The Cuyahoga had experienced such fires at least a half-a-dozen times before this, as had other rivers around the country. Larger fires had often caused considerable damage to docks, ships, and other industrial properties along riverbanks.

Although this was a minor Cleveland occurrence, it made national news because it was mentioned in a Time Magazine article featuring the environment. This was the same issue that carried news of Ted Kennedy's Chappaquiddick incident and the moon landing, making it a widely read issue. So, while it may have been unfair to Cleveland, the story about the burning Cuyahoga became a symbol for the environmental movement. The ensuing furor led to creation of the Environmental Protection Agency and, eventually, the Clean Water Act.

Then by the 1990s, the big argument began about global warming. Was it real, or was the earth just under-going a normal cyclical change? In geological terms, the earth has undergone several ice ages, with mild temperatures in between. At this writing, scientists and politicians still can't agree on the causes or extent of global warming or what we should do about it.

Then there was the oil shortage of the 1970s, and we're still dealing with the effects of foreign-sourced oil. It's ironic that conservation has come full circle. While Muir and Seton and others got Americans to think about conserving the wilderness, instead of just applying the term conservation to industrial/ commercial supplies, we're back to primarily focusing on air, water, oil, and related resources. Should we drill for more oil, or should we protect the wilderness and the waterways and just learn to use less? If we drill, where should we drill, and what will be the impact on the environment and wildlife?

Meanwhile, the concern about saving wilderness areas and wildlife has almost become secondary—or tertiary. This is where we are as this book is being written. When we are faced with economic recession, in addition to energy source limitations, suddenly wildlife preservation doesn't seem quite as important.

This changing of priorities can be quite damaging. If we lose our wilderness areas, they will be gone forever. We can't allow that to happen!

Cleveland Metroparks —The System that Made Look About Lodge Possible

"Parks Should Preserve the Environment as Guardians, Rather Than As Gardeners."

—*Adolph Murie*

To understand today's Look About Lodge, it is helpful to not only understand the conservation movement and the National Parks, but you also need to understand the background of Cleveland Metroparks.

Cleveland Metroparks is known as Cleveland's "Emerald Necklace." It is a ring of natural forests and meadows that encircles Greater Cleveland on three sides. Lake Erie, part of the Great Lakes natural phenomenon, provides Cleveland's northern border. Cleveland Metroparks is dedicated to conservation, education, and recreation.

After World War I, the nation was ready for a new focus. This was, in part, the reason for the funding of Cleveland Metroparks and why The Cleveland Natural Science Club came into being.

Cleveland Metroparks was formally established on July 23, 1917, "to provide open space for the people of Greater Cleveland, as well as to conserve and preserve the natural valleys of the area." Cleveland Metroparks became the state's first municipal park system, and is still its largest.

The seed for a Cleveland park system was planted in 1905 when William Stinchcomb, a self-taught engineer, floated the idea of an emerald necklace to the City of Cleveland. He tried again in 1909. At that time, Cleveland was the nation's sixth largest city.

Everything seems to depend on politicians. In 1911, the Ohio Senate passed a bill authorizing the creation of park boards and empowering them to receive gifts of land. However, they neglected to give park boards authorization to seek operating funds.

There is no record of why William Stinchcomb came up with the "Emerald Necklace" concept. As a self-taught man, he probably read the writings of Muir, Seton, and Roosevelt— and even Burroughs. At the time, he had been elected Cuyahoga County Engineer. Stinchcomb envisioned parkland surrounding Cuyahoga County, and connected by a continuous parkway.

In 1915, Fredrick Law Olmsted, a landscape architect with a national reputation, came to explore the valleys of the Rocky River, Chagrin River, Euclid Creek, and others in the area that were surrounded by woodlands. Olmsted's studies were the basis of the Park District's first task—to acquire land.

Finally, in 1920, the State legislators passed legislation authorizing park boards to get operational funding through tax levies. In 1921, William Stinchcomb was named the park district's first director.

Rapid Growth

From an initial 109 acres of land in the Rocky River valley set aside in 1917, by 1921 the Park's land holdings had reached one thousand acres, and by 1930, the Park District had grown to nine thousand acres of land in nine reservations. By 1950, the Park District held title to over thirteen thousand acres, and by 1992, its seventy-fifth anniversary year, the System boasted just over nineteen thousand acres of land in twelve reservations.

The Park Board's primary job initially was to set aside acres of land for the citizens, and to do so before Cleveland's urban expansion raised prices and made the land unattainable. The board's next task was to make the land available to the public. This was done with improvement projects that began with roads and included picnic areas, hiking trails, baseball diamonds, and summer campsites, and a very vital task was to acquaint the public with the possibilities of Park development. Much of the land that was acquired for parks had been cleared for farmland, so reforestation with native species was initiated.

In 1926, a nine-hole golf course was opened at Mastick and Lorain Roads. It became very popular as the west side's first public course. In addition, a dam was built in Hinkley, flooding one hundred acres for fishing and swimming.

With guidance from the Natural History Museum and help from the Boy Scouts and Cleveland Natural Science Club, nature trails were established in the Cleveland Metroparks reservations. The first hiking trails were completed in 1922 in the Rocky River and Brecksville Reservations. The Cleveland Natural Science Club soon established nature trails in the Bedford and South Chagrin Reservations.

In 1929, the nine reservations were still separate and unconnected, so another priority became connecting them—into a string of pearls (or emeralds).

In 1930, The Cleveland Museum of Natural History gave Dr. Arthur B. Williams the *special assignment* of naturalist for the Cleveland Metropolitan Park Board.[38] His job was to interpret the plant and animal life in the 9,700 acre Park District. He spent much of his first year as naturalist in researching and understanding the natural history of the Park District's reservations. This laid the groundwork for intensive studies that formed the foundation of the Metroparks' program of structured but informal outdoor education and interpretation.

In March, 1930, the Cleveland Natural Science Club completed laying out a nature trail in Bedford Glens. It was visited by six hundred invited guests and by classes from Western Reserve University. Permanent labels were placed on trees and shrubs and seasonal labels placed by flowers. Also, interesting geological features were labeled.

During the depression of the 1930s, tax receipts declined, threatening the park district's existence. Park labor worked at reduced hours and the work was spread around to keep all employees working. However, in the Park Board's Report of activities in 1931, they revealed that so great had been this increase in park attendance "that all methods formerly employed to estimate attendance have entirely broken down, and it is impractical to even hazard an estimate which could be sustained. It is safe to say that the estimated attendance of two million in 1930 was far exceeded in 1931."

There were two reasons for this phenomenal interest in the Cleveland Metroparks. "The first is undoubtedly that the system and its facilities for recreation and education were becoming better known. Park upgrades had expanded facilities, lessoned congestion, and encouraged attendance. "In addition, the employment conditions during 1931 (in the Great Depression) had left people with enforced idle time on their hands. The parks were readily at hand, and there are no charges for their use. The entire family could enjoy the Parks together."

Another Cleveland Metroparks policy change in 1931 was the diversion of money intended for the purchase of land to the hiring of men. To spread this benefit among as many as possible, the workday and workweek length were reduced, allowing for an increase in the number of workers. As a result of the increased manpower, many pending improvements were completed. This made an important impact on the services provided. Cooperation with the Cleveland Museum of Natural History continued, and two small trailside museums were erected—one in the North Chagrin Reservation and one in the Rocky River Reservation.

A third was built in the Brecksville Reservation, with work contributed by both CCC and WPA Federal assistance. The Brecksville Museum was completed in 1939, just a year after today's Look About Lodge. Each trailside museum had a *council ring* where lectures were given, as did Look About Lodge.

As the economic depression extended into 1932, over four million visitors came to the Cleveland Metroparks reservations annually. People who had formally traveled throughout the country for recreation and summer vacations instead visited the Cleveland Metroparks. This compares with two million total National Park visitors in 1931 for all of the national parks in the US, thus demonstrating the value of metropolitan parks. A statistical analysis showed that the majority of pleasure driving was within thirty miles of the drivers' home.

In 1932 to 1933, a new trail was built to access Squaw Rock in the South Chagrin Reservation. As one of the most beautiful in the Cleveland Metroparks System, the trail follows the rock outcroppings along the Chagrin River's bank. Early industry was represented in the Reservation by the development of the Quarry Rock area, an old whetstone quarry site.

Five nature trails were maintained in the Cleveland Metroparks during 1933—three in cooperation with the Cleveland Museum of Natural History and two by the Cleveland Natural Science Club. The nature trails were used and viewed by thousands of park visitors.

Recognizing the value of educational programs provided by the Cleveland Natural Science Club on a volunteer basis, in 1954, Cleveland Metroparks invested in a full-time naturalist, including support staff. The new department was headed by Harold E. Wallin, Park Naturalist.

Initially, Wallin's support staff was a single secretary. Then, in 1972, he was allowed to hire several part-time naturalists. By 1982, when Robert Hinkle became Chief Naturalist, there were three full-time naturalists at North Chagrin, and two each at Rocky River and Brecksville, plus two part-time naturalists.

Today, Cleveland Metroparks' comprises over 22,000 acres of land in sixteen reservations, plus the Cleveland Metroparks Zoo. A series of parkways connects most of the reservations, thereby providing the thread of the necklace.

In addition to its wildlife habitat and wilderness set-aside, Cleveland Metroparks has received recognition numerous times by national and state agencies. These include the National Association of Interpretation, the National Parks and Recreation Association, and the Ohio Parks and Recreation Association. Cleveland Metroparks has received the prestigious Gold Medal Award from the National Parks and Recreation Association three times, most recently in 2008. It can be argued that current award winning education program grew out of the early educational activities of the Cleveland Natural Science Club.

In 2009, there were forty full-time, part-time, and seasonal naturalists on staff. The professional staff was augmented by four cultural history interpreters, five education specialists, eighteen recreational specialists, and backed up with twenty-four other support staff members. Numerous volunteer assistants helped out during programs.

Seasonal naturalists are added during the summer. This enabled Cleveland Metroparks to provide natural science interpretation programs to 3,533,518 children and adults in 2009.

So, now that you have some background, let's get back to the original subject of this treatise—Look About Lodge. Let's take a look at the relatively short history of the Look About Lodges, at the time of this writing just about eighty years.

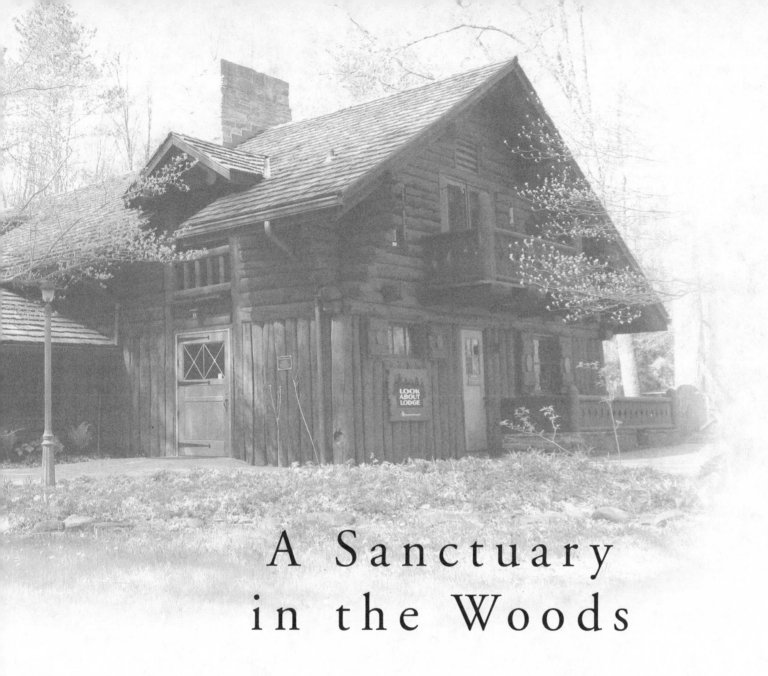

A Sanctuary
in the Woods

The First Look About Lodge

"Study nature, love nature, stay close to nature. It will never fail you."

—*Frank Lloyd Wright*

Yes, I did say, "Look About Lodges!"

In the spring of 1931, "a few very wet and bedraggled members [of the Cleveland Natural Science Club] had their first glimpse of the little old farmhouse at the corner of Solon and River Roads in Bentleyville Village."[39] Called the Winslow house, the building was in a rural—and natural—setting on land that had been acquired by Cleveland Metroparks. According to Edna Wooley, Club members "loved the place at first sight, and it was a day of real jubilation."

On June 6 of 1931, the Cleveland Metroparks Board gave the old farmhouse to the Club for its use "on condition that the place should be repaired and kept in good order by the organization, and that the Club provide educational programs to the public. In addition, the Club was asked to make an annual report to the Park Board of the activities at the facility so they could be added to the Park Board's Annual Report to the public."

As previously mentioned, the Science Club adopted the building as its clubhouse and named it Look-About-Lodge. In addition to making room for meetings of up to one hundred people, the Club developed a natural sciences library and a small museum, similar to those in the trailside museums located in other Cleveland Metroparks reservations. Oil lamps were used for lighting in the Lodge. Outside, they had a council fire pit, as did the trailside museums.

According to the 1932 to 1933 Park Commissioners Annual Report, "The house was given a new roof, plus painted both inside and out. A picnic table had been set under the cherished apple tree, and an outdoor stove was built near the powwow center.

"The grounds have been turned into a colonial garden. Meandering from one corner of the garden down through the woods and along the Chagrin River bank and homeward over the meadow goes the Club's private nature trail zigzagging to include all kinds of natural specimens. The key to this trail hung on the living room wall in the Lodge. It was a large map on which water color drawings and photographs locate the true route to follow. Expenses incidental to the use of this property are all borne by the Club.

"During the last year (1932), more than 1,200 persons have been guests at the facility."

The 1934 to 1935 report included, "During the year, hundreds of persons as guests of Club members have availed themselves of the luxury of the wide old porch, wandered over the Club's trail in the woods, strolled through the Colonial garden adjoining the Lodge, cooked their meals over an outdoor stove, picnicked under the old apple tree in the yard, sung around a campfire, and learned to identify constellations on starry nights.

"There have been lectures, amateur and professional motion pictures, fraternal and scholastic reunions, faculty picnics, and family parties. There have been guests from the Pacific and Atlantic coasts, and from old Mexico. There have been guests with more than one college degree, and there have been guests who were hearing for the first time that all maple trees do not yield sap that makes good maple syrup, or that stars do not twinkle.

"To estimate the value of Look About Lodge is not difficult when one realizes that never has a guest gone away without a deeper appreciation of the natural sciences, of the need for intelligent teaching of conservation, and of the cooperation between the Park Board and this organization of natural science teachers and students."

A Historic Farmhouse

President William McKinley's sister-in-law had lived in the Winslow house. Subsequently, it became an orphanage for Bentleyville Township. One Chagrin Falls resident remembers going to school in a little white building across the road from the farmhouse. By 1932, that school building had become the town hall of Bentleyville Village.

Edna Wooley also wrote, "There is evidence that at least part [of the farmhouse] was built in pioneer days when lumber was sawed and hewed by hand. The ceiling beams are so low that a six-footer has to walk about with a respectfully bowed head. There is no decay evident in the wood of that part of the house, but in the newer part dry rot had made the beams unsafe so the club had to reinforce them."

In addition to upgrading the building, the Club made improvements to the grounds. One such activity was a colonial garden, created to exhibit various plants that could be used in home gardens and on city lots throughout Cleveland and its suburbs.

A Service Tradition

In Ellis Persing's[40] words, "The Science Club needed a building for its headquarters and program activities. Representatives of the Park Board offered us the use of the old Winslow farmhouse. If the club maintained the building, and provided educational programs for the public, it was rent-free, since this was a cooperative venture.

"We accepted and repaired the building, cleaned the well, put in a new pump, landscaped the grounds (with a donation of shrubs), and laid out the Colonial Gardens. These facilities seemed to serve our needs for several years.

"Before the Science Club took up residence in South Chagrin, members had laid out the original Bedford Reservation Nature Trail and maintained it. In addition, they created and maintained a public Nature Trail in the South Chagrin Reservation."

According to Edna Wooley, "Members worked hard to fulfill their building occupancy obligations, improving the building and surrounding land so it became a credit to the Park Board."

This venture was so successful that it initiated a Cleveland Metroparks Board policy of turning over unoccupied buildings on park property to qualified organizations to use and improve. This avoided the need to tear down historic buildings that were

on land acquired by Cleveland Metroparks. Remember that this was 1931 in the early years of the Great Depression.

Edna Wooley continued, "One of the later residents had installed a furnace, a bathroom, and a water tank with a pump to keep the tank filled. In the kitchen is an old iron sink with a pump, and a modern white enamel sink that is provided with hot and cold water faucets. Outside is a well of excellent water. The Club carries water from the well, rather than repair the more modern devices, and for occupation of the Lodge on cold days, it installed a big old-fashioned heater and put the old living-room fireplace into shape for use. Oil lamps furnish the lighting. The old atmosphere has been preserved as far as possible.

"In the kitchen, however, is a four-burner oil range on which the cooking is done when (use of the) outdoor fire was not desirable."

Nature Appreciation Through Education and Conservation

During their tenure at the original Look About Lodge, the Club maintained an active schedule of nature-based activities, both at the Lodge and beyond. Some examples of these activities, taken from the remaining Club Bulletins (its newsletter) and the Annual Reports to the Park Board, include:

➤ **The First Tree Planting Day** was held on April 23, 1932 and became an annual tradition thereafter.

➤ **Permanent VP:** On February 12, 1932, the position of "Permanent Vice President was established and awarded to Ellis Persing in recognition for his part in founding and growing the Club.

➤ **Sections Address Special Interests:** The Club formed separate sections around special interests. Section Q was for junior members, and included sixty students from Western Reserve University. Section X was the travel group, and Section K focused on photography.

➤ **The Colonial Garden:** As part of its mission to upgrade the building and grounds, the Club decided to create a colonial garden with native plants, thereby enabling the garden to serve an educational purpose. They enlisted the help of the Cleveland Metroparks landscape architect, William Munson, to design and lay out the garden. The flower beds were outlined with bricks, and the paths graveled.

After conferring with the Science Club's officers, Munson "drew a plan partly to celebrate the Washington bicentennial year and partly to be in keeping with the age of the Lodge building, which was something more than a century old."

"Planting was begun in April of 1933, on the first anniversary of acquiring Look About Lodge." Some of the 150 plants and shrubbery were purchased, and some were donated. The garden was created about one hundred feet from the Lodge. Many of the original shrubs, rose vines, and trees near the building were retained."

In 1936, members were invited to maintain their own plot in the colonial garden. This meant primarily planting annuals among the perennials each year and keeping the plot weeded.

As Edna Wooley described it, "The Colonial Garden is really an ambitious undertaking, but the almost two hundred science students and teachers comprising the club membership ought to be able to handle it well under Mr. Munson's guidance. In time, it will be a 'show place' for visitors. By that time, the Lodge will have a new coat of paint also—which is very much needed."

➤ **A Private Nature Trail:** Architect Munson also suggested a private nature trail leading from the garden into the woods and on down to the Chagrin River. It was scientifically laid and marked by the Club. A map of the hidden trail hung on the living room wall inside the Lodge. A bulletin was created listing more than one hundred trees, shrubs, and wild flowers on the trail. It provided the common name, scientific name, and characteristics of each.

This was in addition to the nature trail the Club had created and was maintaining in the Bedford Reservation. The Bedford trail was inspected weekly, with tree, shrub, and flower labels kept current as the seasons changed.

In addition to the Lodge and the garden, the grounds included an outdoor stove with picnic tables under an old apple tree, as well as a campfire area. During 1934, over 1,500 persons enjoyed the Lodge and its grounds. This included members, guests, and the public. Groups of up to one hundred persons attended special programs.

On June 8, 1935, the Club accepted an Alaskan totem pole as a gift from Ellis Persing. The purchase was arranged through the Canadian Pacific Railway. The six-foot tall totem cost sixty dollars, plus $7.50 for shipping, and still stands above the south fireplace in today's Look About Lodge.

The first article in the October 6, 1935 Bulletin read:
"This Bulletin comes to acquaint you with Club activities; it is one of the services for which you pay when you pay your dues. Thrifty souls read it just as matter of getting their money's worth or of following up their expenditures. Persons who are in the habit of throwing their money away are in the habit of throwing the Bulletin into the waste basket. For the first group, the Club tries to make the Bulletin a reliable messenger. For the second group, the Club can do nothing."

In February of 1936, the Club's Section K (photography) began circulating its subscription copies of photographic magazines among members. (Remember, this was in the middle of the Great Depression.)

In addition to Look About Lodge based activities, other Science Club events included visits to other Metroparks Reservations. In October of 1932, the Club sponsored a trip to the Brecksville Reservation of Cleveland Metroparks for "an incredible view of fall colors." After the tour, the group went to the Spanish Tavern for one dollar per plate dinner.

On October 28, 1932, the Club sponsored its first annual luncheon for the Northeast Ohio Teachers' Association which met in Cleveland every fall. This became an annual occurrence.

The Club also sponsored two to three educational field trips each year. These were sometimes called "Round Abouts." The first in a series of such trips was made on September 30, 1933, no mention of where they went. In October of 1935, the Club sponsored a trip to Cook Forest Park in Pennsylvania. This is a 7,182 acre National Natural Landmark located in Western Pennsylvania on the Clarion River near the Alleghany National Forest.

The Club also sponsored a trip to Dearborn, Michigan, in the fall of 1935. They visited Greenfield Village where they viewed replicas of Henry Ford's factory and Thomas Edison's Menlo Park, New Jersey, Laboratory. While there, of course they also visited the Detroit Zoo—at the time, one of the country's best.

On November 30, 1935, members and the public went on a "Holiday Hike," the second in that year's series of sponsored trips to Cleveland Metroparks Reservations. This one was to South Chagrin, and was lead by Cleveland Metroparks Landscape Architect William Munson of the Park Board. It was announced in the Plain Dealer,[41] and the public was invited. The group met at Shaker Square[42] and caravanned to the reservation.

The Annual Dinner and Annual Meeting were combined in 1936. The affair was held at the Chamber of Commerce's Midday Club in downtown Cleveland on January 16. The price of the dinner was $1.35, including tax and tip, of course. That year the speaker was Mr. Ajer of the General Electric Co. His subject was physical science research. According to the Bulletin, "He not only provided

knowledge, he tore down popular misconceptions such as the secret of the firefly's flicker."

An annual sugar bush trip was also a regular affair. In 1936, the trip was to a local Northeast Ohio bush at the farm of member Warren Miller in Fowlers Mills. A friendly warning was given to attendees. "Anyone who comes without warm clothing and galoshes will regret it."

On the Sunday afternoon of April 26, 1936, members and the public met at Shaker Square and again caravanned to South Chagrin Reservation to see and hear about "Seldom Visited Places in South Chagrin Reservation." Park landscape architect Arthur Munson led the hike.

On May 30, 1936, Dr. S. Prentiss Baldwin of Gates Mills opened his bird study laboratory for Club visitors. Wrens were the main feature of that program.

On June 12 to 14, 1936, Club members took an overnight *Round About* to the Heart's Content Scenic Area, a patch of virgin woodland in the Allegheny National Forest of Western Pennsylvania. Overnight lodging at the Sheffield House was one dollar for double occupancy. Section K (the photographic section of the Club) used this excursion as its regular meeting date for the month.

There was an early morning hike and riding party (with real horses) on Sunday morning, September 12, 1937. It was a chance to view nature from a new perspective. Breakfast was served for thirty-five cents a plate at nine o'clock in the morning. Reservations were required.

Taking time for Recreation

On November 14, 1931, the Club held the First Benefit Bridge Party at Higbee's Lounge and Silver Grille.[43] This party and fundraiser became a tradition during November that went on for many years. It was billed as a way to repay friends for a social obligation. It was also a fundraiser. Several other card parties were held throughout the year, but the one in November in Higbee's Lounge was the big one. There was also an annual "Spring" card party at the Lodge, usually in June.

On December 6, 1934, the men of the Club held a stag dinner at the Lodge. The purpose was to initiate a Men's Section for the Club. As a Club founded by teachers, the majority of its members were women. However, this mix changed as the Club grew.

The Club usually held a Halloween Party each year. Costumes were worn, and pumpkin pie, coffee, popcorn balls, and favors were provided for twenty cents. In 1935, it was a bring-your-own-supper affair held on November 2nd.

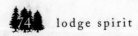

A Unique New Look About Lodge
—A Cooperative Venture

"This time, like all times, is a very good time, if we but know what to do with it!"

—*Charles H. Kettering*[44]

As the club's membership grew, the Bentleyville farmhouse became inadequate. William A. Stinchcomb, Cleveland Metroparks' Executive Secretary, and the Cleveland Metroparks Board gave the Science Club the privilege of choosing a site in the South Chagrin Reservation, where a new and permanent clubhouse could be built. In 1935, the Park Board's Landscape Architect, Arthur Munson, joined with Prof. Persing to begin searching for and selecting a new site.

The Park Board wasn't able to contribute funds directly to construction of the Lodge, because the building was to be used exclusively by the Science Club. The building, on park land, would be owned by the Park Board. Similar arrangements were made in building the Playhouse Settlement Camp in the Brecksville Reservation and another building being constructed in the Rocky River Reservation for use by another social organization, so the Science Club arrangement was the forerunner, but not a unique one.

For its first fifty-five years, the new Lodge was maintained by, and the responsibility of, the Cleveland Natural Science Club. In Ellis Persing's words,

"In the meantime, the old house needed costly repairs, and, obviously, it was too small as the membership increased. In a series of informal conversations with Park Board representatives, the idea of a new structure was conceived.

"We were encouraged (without a written formal contract, which would have been impossible at the time) to sound out the membership about the advisability of attempting to build a meeting place. The membership gave me the green light, and in 1935 an architect was employed. Plans were prepared and submitted to a Science Club committee and the Park Board for approval.

"The original plan, as I remember, was to completely finance the building on Park land (instead of purchasing a lot and building our own Lodge). About that time, there seemed to be a possibility of securing WPA labor for a building on public land, (if the Park would also supply some labor), so the Science Club agreed to purchase materials with the understanding that the Club would have the sole right to use of the building to develop their educational programs.

"I went to the membership for the funds as estimated. The amount was subscribed and loan certificates were issued, non-interest bearing. (Later, these notes were paid off to holders of certificates where desired, but most of these were turned in as donations.)

"Since the labor was available, we were able to enlarge (the Lodge plan), and add more features such as chandeliers (hand made), settees, etc. We secured the materials. A second request brought donations from five dollars to twenty dollars.

"This reduced our responsibility to upkeep and an educational program. Our obligation was also maintenance on a year-by-year basis.

"It seems some people cannot understand why and how we got the building. The answer is The Park Administration had faith in somebody.

"I had an idea. I found people who had faith:

"Who Built the Lodge? The Park Board.

"Who owns the Lodge? The Park Board.

"By what right does CNSC occupy the Lodge? Park Board permit.

"Why was the permit granted?

"By virtue of CNSC Public Service:

a) Maintaining a Nature Trail
b) Providing Educational Programs to the public
c) Promoting Conservation and Science Education.

"What financial consideration allowed granting of the permit?

a) Maintenance of the Building & Grounds by CNSC
b) Insurance paid by CNSC"

As one of its responsibilities, the Science Club sent an annual report of its activities and of park visitors served to the Park Board. The response was a legal document titled, "A Camp Permit to Occupy the Lodge." The first one for the new Lodge was dated April 9, 1938.

In 1937, Ellis Persing described the purpose of the new Lodge: "The new Lodge will make possible an extended type of service to the individual members who in turn will render an ever larger service to the children in the schools and the community."

Membership cards were made to identify Science Club members to Cleveland Metroparks' police who were responsible for security at the Lodge.

The Setting

One site considered was on the Winslow farmhouse Look About Lodge property, which was on the edge of the South Chagrin Reservation, but the building could not "be placed to advantage" there. It made sense to select the new site in the same area. Club members were familiar with this section of South Chagrin, because they had created nature trails there.

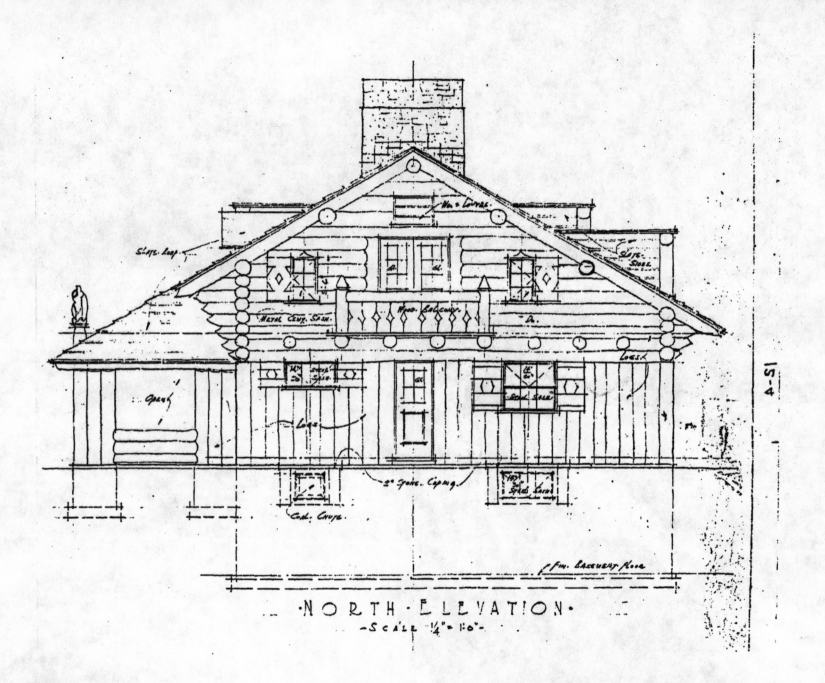

NORTH · ELEVATION

-SCALE ¼" = 1'0"-

On October 21, 1936, Mr. Munson and Professor Persing selected the present site for the new Look About Lodge. The site was secluded, but highly accessible. In addition, the area was rich in biological and geological materials.

For perspective, consider how Margaret Suhr Reed compared the North and South Chagrin Reservations in a 1945 Cleveland Press[45] article. (This was published some seven years after the new Lodge was completed.) "The South Chagrin Reservation is not so well known. Those people who are just now discovering it for the first time are promising themselves many more hours there. It is wilder and more rugged than the North Chagrin Reservation.

"A well marked trail, maintained by the Cleveland Natural Science Club, through the cool shade around the river, over rocks and around rippling falls, and the picnic tables and stoves, are about the only marks of man's intrusion there."

The Architect

Anton George Nosek Jr., a young architect with an Austrian heritage,[46] was selected to design the unique multi-purpose clubhouse. Nosek had graduated from the Cornell University's School of Architecture in 1925. He designed a variety of buildings for Cleveland Metroparks during the 1930s and thereafter.

His daughter credits Cleveland Metroparks work for "putting food on the table" during the Great Depression. A list of the other Cleveland Metroparks' buildings that he designed during the 1930s, and that are still standing, is provided in Appendix H.

One WPA project designed by Anton Nosek for the Cleveland Metroparks was the Shelter House on Hawthorn Parkway (just east of Sulphur Springs Drive). This is the largest shelter house in the Cleveland Metroparks. He continued designing buildings for Cleveland Metroparks through 1968.

Design and Construction

Ellis Persing and the Science Club Board chose Old Faithful Lodge in Yellowstone National Park as the basis for the design of the new Look About Lodge. A number of Club members had been to Yellowstone and had visited Old Faithful Lodge.

Lodge blueprints were initially submitted on August 21, 1935, with revisions completed on March 26, 1936. The WPA Project Proposal was submitted on January 6, 1936.

In February of 1936, as the new Lodge was becoming a reality, members were asked to submit the monies that they had been pledged and agreed to loan for the new clubhouse. About one hundred of the two hundred members responded with funds.

Old Faithful Lodge, Yellowstone

Creative Financing

The May, 1936 Bulletin reported that several Club members had entertained groups of non–member friends in their homes with the objective of obtaining additional subscriptions for financing the new Lodge. All members were encouraged to do so.

The Cleveland Natural Science Club had not yet become a *not-for-profit* corporation, so the purchase of the materials, as well as the proposal for WPA funds, was submitted by the Cleveland Metropolitan Park District. The Science Club then reimbursed the Park District for the cost of the building materials.

The new Look About Lodge was built from 309 American chestnut logs totaling over five thousand linear feet. The logs had a minimum diameter of twelve inches, and cost twenty-two cents per linear foot.

Irving C. Geist, supplier of the roofing slate learned that the Club was financing the building through donations and bonds. He thus offered a discount of two dollars per square, which amounted to seventy-five or eighty dollars on the order.

He promised "a material of character and quality fitting the specific building. In other words, please think of this as Antique Slate and not as second hand or reclaimed." Thus, this was another early example of recycling.

The new Lodge was built primarily during 1937 and 1938. Mr. Munson, Prof. Persing, and "Tony" Nosek constantly supervised the construction of the building.

The Lodge atmosphere has always been special. It offers a respite from problems in the economy and the world. Especially during the earlier years, a love of nature brought Science Club members, and many visitors, to the Lodge frequently.

The Investment

The WPA Lodge grant was a portion of $206,637 in total WPA funding invested in the Cleveland Metroparks during 1936 and 1937.

Financing and operation of the new Lodge was the Science Club's responsibility. The WPA labor was a great help, but a significant investment was still needed from Club members for the building materials and furnishings.

The total construction investment, according to the WPA proposal, was $16,327. While the labor to build the Lodge was largely provided by the WPA grant of $11,344, the remaining $4,983 for construction materials was funded by the Science Club's membership from loans and gifts.

The Science Club's membership thus paid for the building's design, construction materials, its furnishings, and all operating expenses.

As the Bulletin editor put it, "However, even elastic snaps if stretched too far. There's the furnace, and the Mother Hubbard cupboard that needs to be filled with dishes."

Again. this was during the Great Depression. In addition, most members were teachers, and thus didn't generate a great deal of personal wealth. So, Ellis Persing and the building committee came up with a plan.

On October 18, 1935, Ellis Persing asked members to make a loan of ten dollars, and later a donation of five dollars, to finance the new Lodge. All but fifty of the Club's two hundred plus members responded.

The budget projection showed that if two hundred members responded, the Club could meet its financial obligations. Benefit Bridge Parties were scheduled, and raffles were held for donated gifts.

According to the Park Board Report of 1938, the Club contributed approximately $8,500 toward materials and furnishings. With the loans and donations, plus the Club's treasury, it was projected the Club could invest about ten thousand dollars in the new Lodge.

A three page flyer was created to promote the benefits of the new Lodge. Lodge features, plus some fourteen activities and three Club sections were listed as benefits. This included national organization affiliations. Excerpts from the flyer follow:

"What you are able to enjoy for three dollar dues"

New Lodge—for Club activities, built of chestnut logs.

Kitchen—Convenient, hot and cold running water.

Assembly Room—For Club programs and meetings, with two large stone fireplaces and electric lights.

East Porch—Sixty by twelve feet and screened for rest and observation.

South Porch (ground level)—twelve by twenty-four feet for quiet, rest, and general use.

Sun and Observation Porch (second floor)—Above the south ground level porch, this will be used for reading and observation.

Rest Room—with modern equipment.

Library, Lounge, and Museum—Thirty-six by sixteen feet with a stone fireplace for study, reading, meetings, and relaxation.

Basement—Furnace, coal room, storage, and a photographic darkroom.

Parking—Adequate space for sixty cars and flood lit.

Outdoor Stove—Stone fireplace or stove for cooking. Ample for four groups.

Amphitheatre and Campfire Site—Outdoor meeting place for lectures, movies, and campfires.

Playground (west lawn)—Large open space for games.

Arboretum and Gardens—Native plants will be labeled about the Lodge. Exotic plants will be introduced. A wild flower garden is planned and also an herb garden.

Motion Picture Projector and Films—A 16mm motion picture projector is available for use by members. Take the projector home and entertain your friends. An extensive catalogue of films is available.

Trail Activities—South Chagrin Nature Trail maintained for the Cleveland Metropolitan Park Board. Here is an opportunity to gain experience in identifying and labeling wild flowers, trees, shrubs, mosses, ferns, club mosses, algae, fungi, rocks, insects, etc.

The Builders

As mentioned previously, unique circumstances enabled the Lodge to be built during the Great Depression of the 1930s. The construction work was done with WPA labor. These workers were skilled craftsmen, most of whom lived in the area and couldn't find work due to the economic hard times.

During this same period, the CCC (Civilian Conservation Corps) was also formed to provide gainful employment during the Depression. They planted pine trees throughout the Metroparks.

LOOK
ABOUT
LODGE

Cleveland Metroparks

Front Gate

Taking a break in the kitchen window

The Structure

As previously mentioned, Look About Lodge was built from 309 American chestnut logs, totaling over five thousand linear feet. In addition to forming the exterior walls, these logs were used in the staircases leading from the assembly room.

The files contain a list of suppliers who quoted on providing the logs. One offered southern pine, while another offered red cedar telephone poles. A sufficient number of American chestnut logs was finally located in a tree grove near Loudonville, Ohio (in Medina County about sixty miles southwest of the Lodge).

When considering the reasons for selecting American chestnut, the choice was an appropriate one; they grew to between seventy and one hundred feet tall. Through the 1800s, the mighty American chestnut trees comprised about 25 percent of the deciduous forests from Maine to Florida and west to central Indiana. The wood was unique because it was knot-free to a tree height of seventy feet and easily worked.

But, in the late 1800s, a fungus blight began decimating these giant trees. They then had to be harvested while the wood was still useful. However, due to the economic depression of the 1930s, the demand for building products was limited.

Thus, American chestnut logs were an ideal building material—particularly for a nature study lodge. This was a true example of conservation, or of recycling natural resources—and in this case, for the benefit of nature!

The Science Club board was excited about their new building. In June of 1937, about half way through the Lodge's construction, an article in the Bulletin implored, "Of course, the Lodge is still far from its formal opening, but it is a wonderful sight even in its present state. The committee invites everyone who has not seen it to go out at once."

A Grand Opening

By the spring of 1938, the new Look About Lodge building was essentially complete. An opening ceremony was scheduled and held on June 5. Ellis Persing's dedication speech, which is an excellent summation of the Science Club's history to that point, is reprinted in Appendix I.

The retiring officers of 1937 reported on the several years of construction, the state of the Club, and the new Look About Lodge. Heading the new slate of officers was Ed Doller as president. As an engineer and member of the building committee, Ed was highly qualified to lead the membership through their first full year of residence in the new Lodge.

The Building committee thanked members who had sent in a loan of ten dollars and a gift of five dollars, and asked the members who hadn't responded to please do so. These are the people who made possible the creation of the new Look About Lodge.

Members Become Host Families

In the Bulletin of April 29, 1938, members were asked to serve as hostesses and hosts once the new Lodge was dedicated and "Open to the Public." Meetings were scheduled to familiarize members with the building's operation, and sign-up sheets were circulated to get commitments for a week at a time in the summer plus weekends during the spring and fall.

The Building Committee then created Rules and Regulations, plus a two-page checklist with forty-one items to be checked in eight different areas. The form was to be filled out both when a hostess/host arrived and when they were leaving the Lodge.

The sleeping quarters were in the loft—or museum room— at the north end of the Lodge. A new davenport (financed by collecting tax stamps) folded out into a double bed, and there were several cots for the children. The beds were broken down and folded up for storage during the day. Yes, we had to make up the beds every night, and then tear them down in the morning to be "ready for company."

1937—A Series of Previews

The focus, in 1937, was to finish the new Lodge and prepare for the opening. In addition, plans were made to upgrade many of the Club's programs and activities.

➤ During 1936 and 1937, each Bulletin (newsletter) provided a status report on the new Lodge's progress.

➤ The anticipation was overwhelming. The Club couldn't wait to use their new Lodge, so on June 5, 1937, (a year before the official opening and dedication) long before the new Lodge was ready for occupation, the Club held its Annual Summer Card Party in their new clubhouse.

➤ The new Look About Lodge was the scene of the first annual Star Gazers Party on July 9, 1937 (even though the building was only half finished). The group met outside, so the building wasn't needed.

➤ The Regular WRU Summer School Picnic was held on the new Lodge grounds Thursday, July 22, 1937. Festivities began at three o'clock, and supper was served at five thirty in the evening for forty-five cents to those who made prompt reservations and brought their own dishes.

➤ They Just Couldn't Wait: On November 14, 1937, the Club hosted a tea for one hundred members and guests. According to the Bulletin, "Candles burned on the mantles and logs glowed in the fireplaces." It was a rousing success, despite the need to make tea "on a stove designed to heat a country depot or workman's shanty!"

➤ The 1937, an Annual Business Meeting was held in the new Lodge on December 12th at three o'clock in the afternoon. The roof was on and the fireplaces at each end of the room were going (glowing). Members were encouraged to come and hear reports of the committees and learn "just what advantages are at the disposal of active members."

At that meeting, members voted unanimously to raise annual dues from one dollar and fifty cents to three dollars and to increase the initiation fee to five dollars. Although many of the construction costs had been paid, monies were still needed for the furniture and fixtures.

The Bulletin stated, "To those who have seen the new Lodge, these increases more than justify themselves."[47] It was determined that, based on the Club's budget, operating costs could be met with these increases, plus a few money-making affairs scattered throughout the year.

Forty-seven new members joined the club in 1937 (the year before the new Lodge was dedicated), bringing total membership to 250.

1938—A Really Big Year

Following is a list of some, but not all, of the activities during 1938, the dedication year of today's Look About Lodge.

In January of 1938, the building committee reported that the shutters were hung, and the planting of native shrubbery was under way. It included Hawthorne, dogwood, sumac, and bittersweet.(In January?) The carving and painting of gargoyles was completed, and the wood-carver had begun working on the owls and totem poles.

On February 11, 1938, the "Trail Committee" completed a new nature trail adjacent to the new Lodge. This was four months before the new Lodge was finished and dedicated. The Trail Committee hosted a walk in the winter woods on Saturday, February 19 with a splendid dinner following the hike. (All this happened in a snow storm.)

In the Bulletin of March 1, 1938, members were requested to volunteer their services as hostess/host for a week at a time during the summer and on weekends in the spring and fall.

In 1938, the Annual Dinner was held on March 5, rather than in January, to accommodate the speaker's schedule. The dinner was attended by 180 of the Club's 250 members. It was a turkey dinner held in the Red Room of Hotel Cleveland, and cost one dollar and ninety-five cents.

At the 1938 annual dinner, a raffle was held to fund equipment for the "splendid new dark room." The prize was a Leica camera or one hundred dollars. In those days, a darkroom (with a red light) was needed to develop photographs on chemically treated paper.

The annual sugar bush trip was held on March 12 at the Packard Farm between Lodi and Litchfield, which was the largest sugar maple grove in the state. Eighty members attended the event. (Think about eighty people, or even two groups of forty, trying to squeeze into a steam-filled sugarhouse.) The driving time was estimated to be one to one and a half hours (no freeways). Members could cook their own food in the woods or buy lunch at a new restaurant for thirty-five cents.

On April 29 and May 22, there were inspection tours for the hostesses and hosts who planned to keep the new Lodge open during the summer and fall. They met at the new Lodge to learn about "the intricacies of the furnace, lights, fire extinguishers, and *human nature in wild open spaces*." According to the Bulletin, "Any member still debating the pleasures of spending a weekend at the Lodge as master of ceremonies will be convinced of the real fun to be had."

On May 15, 1938, a bird walk from the shelter house at six thirty was attended by sixty members, followed by wonderful breakfast at eight thirty. The breakfast included coffee, bacon, scrambled eggs, and rolls. Problem was, they saw no birds; they heard many, but saw none! (The leaves were out early that year.) As a culmination to the morning though, the four-sided outdoor fireplace at the Lodge was dedicated.

On May 28, Club members ventured to the Warren Miller farm in Fowlers Mills to view insects, and to gain respect for creatures previously called "bugs."

On June 4, (The day before the Big Day!) the Club held its annual summer card party at the Lodge.

On June 5, 1938, the new Look About Lodge was dedicated! The Bulletin recounted: "The new Lodge speaks so eloquently for itself it leaves human vocabularies weak. In every way, it far exceeds the visions of everybody, even of those who so keenly recognized its need." Ellis Persing's dedication speech is reprinted in Appendix I.

A telephone was installed at the Lodge on June 8, 1938. It was on approval, and would stay "if used frequently enough."

Early on Saturday morning, June 18, 1938, a trip was made to Letchworth State Park in New York. Billed as the "Grand Canyon of the East," this is a 14,350 acre park on the Genesee River. (Of course, it's much shallower and much shorter than the Grand Canyon in Arizona, but it is still spectacular.)

This trip was attended by thirty-two members. It required six hours driving time. Overnight cabins that sleep three could be rented for one dollar and fifty cents per night (but you had to bring your own bedding).

On June 21, 1938, the Club held an open house in their new Lodge for the Wild Flower Club—their first official guests—with a capacity crowd attending.

The host and hostess program kept the Lodge open from June 23, 1938, throughout the summer to help members—and the public—enjoy their visit. In September through December, it was open every Saturday and Sunday from one to six in the evening. Members were invited to enjoy the beauty of the woods and the peacefulness of the Lodge, as well as the photography exhibit in the museum.

On June 26, Park Board architect William Munson gave an educational presentation on landscaping with native plants and trees.

The annual picnic took place at the new Lodge on July 20, with 115 in attendance. Students of Western Reserve's Education College summer session were invited to attend. To make everything complete, there was even a glorious sunset!

On August 10, members entertained their friends at a bridge party (partially to show off the new Lodge and partially to generate a little income).

The outstanding event for the month of September was a program on conservation. On September 24, the Science Club hosted a meeting of all the nature clubs in the Cleveland Area. The highly regarded Dr. H. N. Wheeler, Chief Lecturer of the National Forest Service with thirty-two years of experience in conservation, was the keynote speaker. After his speech, he led a roundtable discussion on conservation, a subject that "was attracting the attention of every forward-looking citizen." As expected, there was a capacity crowd.

An Elementary Science Section was established by the Northeast Ohio Teachers' Association on October 6, 1938. The Cleveland Natural Science Club was recognized as the sponsor of this new section.

On Oct. 15, 1938, an open house was held for the Dean Bailey Hiking Club.

Members were invited to lend materials for display in the museum. However, the Bulletin announced that museum exhibits donated/loaned by members must be approved by the Building Committee.

Trail Committee members were available every Saturday and Sunday during October to give tours of the nature trail around the new Lodge. Tours were open to the public.

A Halloween party, an annual affair, was held on October 29th and was attended by ninety members and guests.

The Folk Dancing section of the Club held its session on November 18th.

In 1938, the big annual November Card Party was held on November 19th, again in Higbee's Lounge.

The Annual Business Meeting was held in the new Lodge on December 12, 1938, with a "slight increase" in dues (fifty cents) on the agenda. Transportation was provided for members who needed it. Over one hundred members showed up.

On December 21, students from Western Reserve's Education College had their Christmas dinner at the university, and then came to the Lodge for a Christmas Celebration. This was the first Christmas party in the new building, and the participants were almost giddy with excitement. The festivities included the burning of the Yule log, caroling, a mummers mask, and folk dancing. Members were invited to attend and refresh college memories.

The Bulletin exclaimed, "Words fail to adequately describe the scene at the Lodge on December 21 when we held our first Christmas party in the new Lodge. Never has it been so beautifully decorated. Under the holly and pine branches, students from the Western Reserve University School of Education presented an entertaining program. Never will we forget the picture made by the carolers, as hooded in red and holding lighted candles they stood on the steps above the Christmas tree and sang the old familiar carols."

Such were some of the events and activities that took place during the year of 1938, the year in which today's Look About Lodge was dedicated.

A Distinctive Building

The new Look About Lodge was constructed from stacked, oakum-chinked, American chestnut logs from Loudonville, Ohio. This gives it a rustic look. The external dimensions are ninety-five feet by fifty-six feet.

The building was constructed with a slate roof. Sandstone (used for the south porch supports) and slate, as well as the chestnut logs, were all local materials.

"The design is clean and horizontal, creating the feel of a building constructed by pioneer artisans. It puts the Lodge in harmony with its natural surroundings and ties it to our country's history."[48]

Lodge Exterior Features

The main entrance faces east, with the parking lot to the north. Above the front door is a small dormer balcony for the second floor museum. A screened porch begins left of the front door and extends along the building's east side.

A lawn slops away from the east porch down a gentle slope to the woods.

When the Lodge was built, you could look across the Chagrin River Valley and watch a sunrise from the east porch. In succeeding years, the trees have grown too tall for that treat.

The east porch is twelve by sixty-two feet, and has a flagstone floor.

Four carvings, crafted by WPA artisans, were mounted on the roof above the porch. Two were of owls and two contained other birds and mammals. When these deteriorated from the weather, they were removed. (The owls survived, and are perched in the assembly room on either side of the south fireplace.)

On the south elevation is an open balcony porch that measures fourteen by twenty-six feet. Its corners are supported by Berea sandstone columns, which were originally topped with WPA-carved gargoyles. This upper porch gives an unobstructed view of the sunset. Below the upper porch is a ground level patio with a stone floor.

The north side of the Lodge faces the parking area. It contains the kitchen door, above which is another small balcony for the second floor museum (now the naturalists' offices).

Next to the kitchen door hangs a cowbell, which serves as the door bell.

There is a railing around a basement level well. The basement well contains exterior stairs down to the basement and a small coal chute door for fuel delivery.

The roofing supplier emphasized the slate was antique material, and not just used roofing. This was another early example of recycling. The roof contains six dormer vents—three facing east and three facing west. These vents have wood

Lodge from the west

Doorbell (Yes, it's a cowbell)

East porch

Gargoyle - unpainted

Gargoyle in winter

 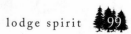

louvers which allow ventilation and promote air circulation in warm weather.

When Cleveland Metroparks took over the Lodge in 1993, the original slate roof had leaks, so it was replaced with a shake roof.

The Lodge was designed to accommodate up to five groups indoors—at each end of the main assembly hall, in the second floor museum, and one at each end of the east porch. An additional three groups could meet outdoors—on the south upper porch, on the south ground level porch, and in the outdoor amphitheater that was beyond the west lawn and next to the four-sided fireplace dining area.

The first floor has fourteen fixed-pane casement windows with steel frames. In the second-floor loft museum are two exterior doors to the dormer porches, two interior doors from the second floor balcony, and three windows. All the buildings windows are framed with stained wood shutters. The larger ones are decorated with hexagons, while the smaller shutters have diamonds.

Lodge Interior Features

"The assembly hall is sixty by twenty-five feet and is built over a crawl space. The hall is two stories high, with walls and ceiling braces of exposed chestnut logs. There are three corner stairways, with split chestnut log stairway risers and log railings. The southwest stairway accesses the south balcony porch. The two north stairs lead to a room width balcony with doors to the museum."

There is a small balcony with a door to the upper porch in the southeast corner of the assembly room. Originally, a fourth stairway was planned for that corner of the room. However, at the suggestion of William Stinchcomb, Cleveland Metroparks Executive Secretary, a book nook replaced the planned southeast stairway.

Stinchcomb took great interest and significant pride in the new Lodge. He would carry a key to the Lodge around with him and would take friends in to view the facility.

The book nook became the location of the Lodge's reference library, providing a book collection for use in interpreting the natural science features of the South Chagrin Reservation.

The assembly hall also contains two large tables made of chestnut wood. These are used for displays or for serving cafeteria-style meals. They originally contained runners made from pieces of silk donated by Club members. This kept down the cost of furnishing, while giving members a more personal feel-

The interior has exposed chestnut walls and beams, varnished floors of maple and pine, plus three sets of stairs with split log risers. The Assembly Hall is the centerpiece of the building. Recent changes have been limited to utility and appliance upgrades, plus safety modifications and building code compliance.

The original furnishings include:

- Iron and punched copper sconces
- Exposed ceiling beams and WPA-constructed cast iron chandeliers
- Chestnut tables
- Half log benches over the heating vents
- Built-in bookcases and cabinets
- A guestbook stand just inside the assembly hall north door to document visitors for Cleveland Metroparks' statistics.

The loft at the north end of the Lodge contained a small museum of educational displays. It was also used for small classes or meetings and as a bedroom for member hosts and hostesses who stayed at the Lodge.

The Memory Stone Fireplace

Members donated a variety of rocks and minerals that they had collected in their travels around the country for use in the loft fireplace. The fireplace represents rocks and minerals from all forty-eight (at the time) states. I guess they were "rock hounds." Thus, this was known as the "memory stone" fireplace. The stones are numbered, and a key identifies their classification, where they were from, and the donating member.

ing of Lodge ownership. One member exclaimed upon entering the assembly hall, "Oh, there's a dress I wore when I went to Alaska."

In the balcony beam above the north fireplace is carved the John Burroughs quote, which exemplifies the Lodge's atmosphere, "I come here often to find myself. It is so easy to get lost in the world."

The north end of the building's ground floor houses an entry hall, a lavatory, the kitchen, and a storage closet, plus steps down to the basement. The museum that was on the second floor is now the naturalists' office.

The basement contains the furnace room and a darkroom. The darkroom was used to create a collection of photos and slides used for nature interpretation.

The six feet tall Thunderbird totem from Alaska. is mounted on the mantle above the south fireplace.

It was given to the Club in 1935 by Ellis Persing

A quote from Chaucer is carved into the beam supporting the landing to the left of the south fireplace: "The lyfe so short, the craft so long to lerne."

A sign stating the Lodge was built by the WPA is above one set of doors from the east porch to the assembly hall.

The southwest stairway accesses the south balcony porch.

Sconce light with copper punched shade

Chestnut bench with heater vents under settees

Kitchen entrance

Ceiling beams with wrought iron straps

One of the two owls that were rescued from the east porch roof, and are now perched next to the south fireplace.

This was, in essence, an extension of the geological exhibit in the display case.

The loft was used as a museum for natural science exhibits. It contains eight double-door display cases. The room was also used as a secondary meeting room and as sleeping quarters for host families.

A beautiful snowy owl under a glass dome was the museum's highlight (but it was taken by villainous hands). There were also collections of mounted butterflies and insects.

The museum cabinets are on each side of the room and contain special lighting to highlight display subjects. A partial list of the museum's permanent exhibits (displayed whenever a "special" exhibit was not mounted) is in Appendix F.

One function of the museum was interpretation of the natural science examples in and around Greater Cleveland, and particularly in the South Chagrin area. Thus, the museum functioned as the South Chagrin Reservation's trailside museum.

The porches were designed as observation porches, and have served a variety of purposes.

East Porch: This 60 ft. long screened porch was, and is, used for numerous activities, including a place for projects like creating leaf prints or other handicrafts.

In 1949, it held the club's exhibit of live animals. It was also used to view recreational activities on the east lawn. This porch was used for picnics during inclement weather or as overflow space for large Science Club dinners.

The Kitchen: In the 1940s, cooking was done on a large coal and wood-burning stove. Initially, food was stored in a real icebox. During the summers, ice was delivered. Just as in Cleveland and its suburbs, a sign was hung in the north kitchen window to let the ice man know a delivery was needed. For functions in the fall, winter, or spring, ice was brought from home by members. Even after the Lodge got an electric stove and a refrigerator, the wood-burner stayed for a while.

In addition to the fireplaces and a wood-burning stove, heat was provided by a large coal-burning furnace in the west side of the basement.

A darkroom was on the east side of the basement steps. (See the description under "Activities.")

South Porches: One was built on the second level above the other, which is a ground level stone floor porch. These were used as additional meeting areas, while the upper porch was used as a star gazing platform and for general observation. In 1963, the upper porch housed the club's bee hives.

The Grounds

When the Lodge was built, the drive culminated close to the kitchen door. It was moved further away in the 1990s to protect the integrity of the building. The coal chute entrance remains under the small fence that surrounds the exterior basement stairs, but the coal bin that was in the basement has been removed.

During the 1940s, the sundial worked (when it wasn't shaded by the trees along Sulphur Springs gorge—or covered with snow). It was located off the southwest corner of the Lodge. (See photo on page 89.)

An Amphitheatre was built just west of the Lodge's entrance drive. Educational presentations were made there (when the weather permitted). Bench seating was whole logs, with the seats facing east. Underground wiring carried electricity from the Lodge to the amphitheatre. There was also a rustic podium, a large screen board was used as picture screen, and there was a stone well for campfires.

Soon after they were installed, the benches became encrusted with partridge tail fungi. But a more irritating problem was the mosquitoes which came out particularly at dusk throughout the summer, due to the vernal pools in the area. Eventually, the benches succumbed to the weather and the amphitheatre was dismantled, allowing the forest to reclaim the area.

The amphitheatre was used as a chapel on some occasions, such as for an Easter sunrise service. One reason may have been the early ties to Epworth-Euclid Church. Most Club members were educated at Western Reserve University or Case Institute of Technology, and Epworth-Euclid sponsored a number of activities for students.

A Four-Sided Stone Fireplace was built just south of the amphitheatre and just beyond the west lawn about eight hundred feet from the Lodge. Tables around the four-sided fireplace were used for individual and Club picnics—breakfasts, lunches, and suppers. The picnic area was designed to handle one hundred to one hundred fifty people.

The four-sided fireplace was apparently a popular design of architect Anthony Nosek. Additional ones are located in several other picnic grounds in the Cleveland Metroparks.

A Rustic Life

Water came from a well just outside the kitchen window, about where the water fountain is today. When the Lodge was built, water was pumped by hand. It had a strong iron taste. Many members thought it tasted great. (I guess I was too used to "city" water.)

Wood and coal were used for cooking in the large kitchen stove. Even after the Lodge got an electric stove, the wood-burning one stayed for a while. As mentioned earlier, the original refrigerator was cooled by blocks of ice, delivered by "The Ice Man," if a sign was left in the window.

When members stayed at the Lodge, bread and milk signs would also be hung in the north kitchen window. These alerted

the route drivers to stop for an order. (This was the same system used for deliveries in Cleveland and its suburbs!)

The building was designed with one small lavatory (but no bath). There were two outhouses at the north end of the parking lot. (Not as handy—or as nice—as the outdoor facilities are today.)

Science Club membership grew in 1937 when forty-seven new members were welcomed (as the new Lodge was being built), bringing membership to 250. Membership reached 275 just after the new Lodge was completed and topped out at about three hundred in the early 1940s.

A Respite

In 1941, the United States was drawn into World War II, and the country emerged from The Great Depression. During this period, the economic challenges included gas rationing and food shortages, as well as a scarcity of other goods and materials.

During the war years, an invitation was made to "come to the Lodge for a morale boost." One guest was quoted as saying, "A day out here makes one forget troubles."

A Bulletin article in 1943 reminded members, "Activities are necessarily curtailed these days (during WWII), but in these times we still need morale builders, and Look About Lodge is still one of the finest places to find one's self.

"The facilities outlined for field day await you every day. Do go out and enjoy the peace and quiet of the woods, browse in the library, or rest on the porch after lunching in the open."

In 1940, the Club welcomed ten thousand visitors into the Lodge throughout the year.

Life and Activities at the Lodge

A Strategic Plan for Use of the Lodge

"Every choice you make has an end result."

—*Zig Ziglar*

At least one attempt was made to establish a plan that would guide the activities of the Club in its new, and much larger capacity, Lodge. Written sometime during the war years (1941 to 1945), today we would call it a strategic plan or a long-range plan.

One purpose of the plan was to maintain an emphasis on education in the natural sciences. There was apparently a concern that with the new building, the Club was over-emphasizing recreational and social activities. The following is from this plan, and is provided to show the importance and use of the Lodge.

Probably written primarily by Ellis Persing, you'll note that it starts out as a standard plan written in third person but becomes a sad first person commentary on the changing priorities of Club members.

"I. Continue to emphasize the educational plan which includes:
Present Plan
1. N.E.O.T.A. Section meeting
2. Membership in American Science Teachers Association
3. Trail Committee
4. Museum Committee
5. Field trips
6. Short courses (omit for duration of WWII)

7. Have one lecture each month during the year and in the city during the winter months, as usual.
8. Annual Dinner, as usual.

New Plan
A. Bird trips in South Chagrin or designated place for the public.
B. Tree and wild flower walks and talks for the public in South Chagrin.
C. Keep the Lodge open fall, spring, and summer, as usual, as long as it is possible because of the war emergency. This allows for an individual to use the Lodge for groups during the week days and for relaxation and study over the weekend.
D. Close the Lodge during December, January, February, and March for the duration. Save fuel and the responsibility of cleaning and janitor service.
E. Do not over emphasize recreation and social until we are able to pay a *part time director.*

"In making a program or planning activities, we must remember, first of all, that we are a science Club and certain activities must claim our attention above everything else. Are we achieving the objectives as set forth by the founders? Some of the older members have been inactive, and many of the new members, during the last several years, fail to carry on along educational lines. Instead, they seem to be more interested in recreational lines and using the Lodge for social activities.

"The museum is vital to the life of the Club. It requires time and thought. It represents the growth and development of the members, as well as the Club. The exhibits help to interpret this area and then spreads to wider and wider areas. [sic] We need scientific background and leadership in this activity. We have had some splendid exhibits in the past. What can we do for the future? How much time and effort can you afford to spend on this feature?

"The trail must be kept up. There is much that can be done beyond the mere routine. The permanent labels should be renewed. The vegetation about the Lodge should be labeled to attract our members and friends. The grounds about the Lodge are rich in plant and animal life. The planting along the walk to the lecture area has been in the making for several years. An herb garden is part of the plan. Can we develop it? We need new and more labels for our trail in winter. Should members of a science club be interested in the out-of-doors in winter? Do we talk to our friends about the trail? Do we go with them to see the seasonal changes?

"For example, the programs in the past have been a service to members. Now could this group take pictures—motion, stills, and natural color—which would be a service to the Club?

"Motion pictures of such activities as Field Day would stimulate members to take advantage of future features. Pictures of the trees, the rocks, and the animals would be most useful for the museum. In fact, one criticism of our photographic exhibit was a lack of biological and natural science subject matter.

"We now have sets of slides in natural color as well as motion pictures which are available for use by members in the home or school. Perhaps such a program is too ambitious.

"There was considerable interest shown for the short courses in Trees in Winter. Insects, etc. I am wondering if we should encourage members to take advantage of such informal courses. One would think members of a science club should want to know more about the trees, the wild flowers, the birds, the insects, the fungi, etc. It would seem this should either be supported or dropped.

"Formerly, field trips were a part of our program and they were well attended. Now one hesitates to ask a leader for fear the number present will not be sufficient to warrant his time. Do we know the story of the rocks of this area? Can we name most of the trees on sight?

"It would seem that members would enjoy frequent trips (informal trips if you wish) just to see the changes that take place during a season out-of-doors. We have some members qualified as leaders and we could secure other competent leaders if conditions warrant. I realize that members need not be scientists but they should have a desire to increase their fund of information.

"Picnics, archery, folk dancing, hiking, and other forms of recreation are merely incidental to the whole Club program. Is there a danger that we over emphasize the recreational phases? We should be able to use the facilities of the Lodge and grounds as long as we do not neglect the educational activities. I am inclined to believe that some of the newer members were attracted by this phase of the Club's activities and do not realize that members should support the educational program.

"We should all realize that we cannot enjoy the recreational and social aspects of the Club unless some few persons make it possible by giving an excessive amount of the time and energy to the educational program. We realize, too, that some members would be happy to contribute more of their time, but their job and home duties will not permit.

"There must also be a plan and one or two persons responsible for the operation of the building and grounds. Certain members have repeatedly said to me, 'Hire someone to do it.' That sounds fine, but it is difficult to do. Up to the present, we have hired some help for cleaning, mowing the lawn, and clerical work. Financially, it was impossible in the past to pay for all the work done. Perhaps in the future we must pay for more of the work since the few people doing it cannot continue. It is also impossible to have just anyone run in and build a fire or work as they happen to be moved by the spirit. The work must be done at a definite time which often is a sacrifice for the person doing it."

One concern probably not realized by many members was that the Club occupied the Lodge on an annual permit basis. A major part of the commitment to Cleveland Metroparks Board was that the Club was to provide an educational program to the public. This was undoubtedly on Ellis Persing's mind.

The following activities and programs are a representative sample of the heavy schedule maintained by the Club. While primarily included to show Lodge-based events, it includes other Club events to provide insight into the diversity of the Club that built Look About Lodge.

Events of the Club That Built the Lodge

"For myself I hold no preferences among flowers, so long as they are wild, free, and spontaneous!"

—*Edward Abbey*

An Emphasis on Education

There were short courses of four to five sessions in length that always included fieldwork.

- Stars
- Conservation
- Beginners Photography
- Advanced Photography
- Geology of South Chagrin
- Insect Identification
- Tree Identification
- Fungi.

Consider how Plain Dealer reporter Margaret Suhr Reed described South Chagrin Reservation in September of 1940—over two years after the new Lodge was dedicated:

"The trail winds through the woods among lacy, sheltering hemlocks and skirts the creek to disclose to an observer the white and snowy spray as it plunges over the layers of Berea grit which forms its bed.

"In one spot ground pine, very rare around Cleveland, like a two-toned crocheted spread covers the ground, and, in another, the waxy leaves of Canadian Mayflowers blot out all traces of the brown earth. Polk milkweed, exquisitely graceful, nods beside the path and false Solomon seals slowly prepare a banquet for the birds that will someday soon repay their hosts by scattering the seeds far and wide. Huckleberries and blueberries also bid for the favor of the winged dwellers of the woods.

"Overhead, a tulip tree whose beautiful beige, peach, and green blossoms are seldom noticed, is protected from the marauding hands of would-be novelty makers. It is a world apart, this trail, a place for peace and refuge."

The Central Association of Science and Mathematics Teachers was entertained by the Club at the Lodge on Saturday, November 23, 1940.

In January of 1941, the monthly Bulletin's name was changed to "The Bypath." Stick figure drawings were added to the masthead and used to illustrate many of the articles.

"Our Galaxy of Stars" was the title of a program on February 1, 1941, given by Dr. J. J. Nassau Director of the Warner and Swasey Observatory of Case School of Applied Science. Dr. Nassau was one of the outstanding astronomers in the country at the time.

An Astronomy Section was formed in the spring of 1941, with the help of Dr. J. J. Nassau and Mr. Russell of the Cleveland Astronomical Society.

On February 15, 1941, the Science Club hosted the Cleveland Chapter of the American Society of Landscape Architects. The group hiked through the woods, and had supper at the Lodge.

On Washington's Birthday in 1941, a trip over the trail began at three o'clock in the afternoon, and a Chow Mien dinner was served at five thirty for thirty-five cents (if fifty or more people show up, or forty cents if there are less than fifty). An evening filled with entertainment rounded out the day."

Wildflower lists were placed on a trail bulletin board during April and May of 1941. The Bypath listed the April blooms that have come and gone as: Hepatica, Spring Beauty, Spring Cress, Trillium, Wild Ginger, Meadow Rue, Rue Anemone, Fawn Lilly, Toothwort, Cut Leaf Toothwort, and Blue Cohosh."

It then pointed out that warm weather brings blossoms out rapidly. "Be looking for Wild Geraniums, Solomon's Seal, Canada Mayflower, Bellwort, Wood Anemone, and Wood Betony. Fruiting bodies on mosses and liverworts could be seen by going down the trail steps and turning left."

The Bypath explained that wildflower blossoms were most prolific in the early spring before the tree leaves formed a canopy over the woods.

On October 4 and 5, 1941, Club members went on a Round About to Wayne Forest and Muskingum Dam, a national forest near Athens, Ohio, to view its natural features.

It was proposed in the November, 1941, Bypath that the November woods may hold little of interest to the botanist, but it can be quite revealing to the geologist. The trail bulletin board described much about the geology of the ground on which the Lodge was built.

On October 19 of 1941, the geology short course took a trip over the nature trail on their fourth and final session. Dr. Arthur B. Williams, Chief Geologist for the Cleveland Museum of Natural History, and on special assignment as Naturalist for Cleveland Metroparks, presented a program on November 9 for Club and public visitors about the geology of the Lodge area.

Photographs from members were mounted in the photographic corner, with ever-changing exhibits.

The 1942 Annual Dinner was held on January 17th in the Guildhall Building. (It had inside parking and an underground passageway into the building.) The speaker was Dr.

E. N. Wheeler, of the US Department of Agriculture's Forest Service. His gave an illustrated lecture on, "Conservation as a War Defense Measure."

Even though the Lodge was closed during February and March of 1942, the Trail Committee was actively preparing for summer. They updated the bulletin boards, gave the label stakes a coat of paint, and transplanted local fauna close to the trail where it could be seen by park visitors.

In March of 1942 (just two months after Dr. Wheeler's speech on "Conservation as a War Defense Measure"), it was decided to cancel all programs at the Lodge during the month of March—to save fuel, tires, lights, etc.

In March of 1942, the government was asking citizens to stay close to home this summer to save gas and tires. The Bypath pointed out that the Lodge was available only a short distance away for picnics and other recreation.

The government suggested having picnics in your own backyard. To do so, it recommended a bulletin on "How to Build an Outdoor Fireplace" which was offered by the US Department of Agriculture.

A full page editorial in the March–April, 1942, issue of the Bypath began with, "Our first objective is to win the war." Lt. General Ben Lear had pointed out in a speech that, "Fighters will win. Some will fight behind guns and on ships, in planes, and in tanks on the ground. Behind them, fighters in factories, on farms, and in offices, on newspapers, in schools, and in every community will help them win."

The editorial reminded members that automobiles should not be used as if it were peacetime. Organizations should, likewise, scale back the activities that draw people to take long trips.

In 1942, the June wildflowers bloomed in May, so the Bypath alerted everyone to come out before they were gone. In addition, those one hundred members and the public who went on the May 3 bird walk found it a bit more difficult to see the birds (due to the woods' canopy).

For the Field Day held on July 18, 1942, members and guests were offered a choice of three different field trips at three thirty in the afternoon. One was on wildflowers, one on insects, and one on snakes, turtles, and birds. A picnic supper was served at five thirty for fifty-five cents with a surprise program scheduled for seven o'clock in the evening. A motion picture on birds *in full color* was shown at eight o'clock.

The Bypath skipped an issue in August, 1942, based on the editorials in previous issues about war-time sacrifices. But, it couldn't resist reminding members of what the Lodge offered in close to home recreation, relaxation, and an excellent place to have a picnic.

In addition to a good stove and picnic tables, the Lodge offered, "a large play area, a well-marked nature trail, a woodland area peopled with many feathered friends, and a splendid museum and library to aid in interpreting what you have seen on the trail. Last but not least, the sunny porches and comfortable lounge invite us to relax and find ourselves."

By September 26, 1942, the Club's membership had expanded to three hundred, so it was decided to have a Founders' Day at the Lodge to get to know each other a little better.

In February of 1943, Ellis Persing asked for members' help in completing the assembly of the Club's new telescope. (An article in the Bulletin pleaded, "Will someone please return the book titled, *How to Assemble a Telescope*.)

A winter hike was taken in Forest Hills Park, in Cleveland Heights, on Feb. 14, 1943. Directions were given for taking the streetcar then walking a few short blocks to the park. Apparently, the winter hike at Forest Hills Park experienced bad weather. (What can you expect in Cleveland on February 14?) So, on Sunday, April 11, 1943, another hike was scheduled. This time, they expected that, "some spring flowers and several feathered friends should be on hand to greet us."

The War was still going on in 1943, so, to celebrate Washington's Birthday, an "in town" program was held at the University Circle Garden Center. The subject was Victory Gardens. It was presented by Henry Prey, Garden Editor of the Cleveland Press.[49]

In 1943, the Annual Spring Bird Hike was scheduled for the first Sunday in May—May 2. Due to food rationing, it was impossible to serve breakfast, so everyone was invited to bring their own. There were fires in the fireplaces, so everyone could cook breakfast and make coffee. It was suggested that members plan to spend the day at the Lodge, which had been closed all winter, to make the "expenditure of gas more profitable,"

A wildflower hike was planned for the afternoon. It turned out to be a cool and rainy day, so the afternoon hike was cancelled. A large group attended, and enjoyed themselves around the fireplaces. It was noted that there was a large carpet of Bluets stretching down the front lawn, and Adder's Tongue lined the driveway. (See photo on page 89.)

A Victory Garden was a vegetable garden in your backyard, or on nearby open land such as a farm. Larger fields of land were divided up to allow people to grow a bigger garden than could be grown in most backyards. (We had a small garden in our backyard, and then another one at a farm about seven miles from home.) Some Victory gardens were also planted at elementary schools.

A guest at the Lodge was quoted as saying, "A day out here makes one forget troubles." The Lodge was kept open with hosts/hostesses during the summer, but some activities were curtailed due to the war.

Still in wartime mode, the annual June card party at the Lodge was held on June 5, 1943. The price was fifty-five cents, including Federal tax.

The Bypath issues were one page during the summer of 1943, and included book reviews plus news of members growing Victory gardens and serving in the military. One-line notes were provided for members' activities, including, "Congratulations to Mrs. Kneale, who was a prize winner at the Harvest Festival." To save paper, the reports of Club committees were spread over several issues of the Bypath.

In September of 1943, a bulletin board was posted at the entrance to the Sulphur Springs trail by member Ethel Young. It told the story of insects to be found there.

The Autumn Open House was held on September 26, 1943. It drew many members and "nature put on quite a show." The Bulletin reported:

"On the path to the fireplace were ladies tresses by the handful. Other bits of beauty were golden rod, milkwort, silver goldenrod, fall asters, and darling little ferns thrusting their clinched fists through the moss. The hillside was dotted with wintergreen, splotched with huckleberry, and highlighted with flames of sumac. There were white crabapples clinging to leafless trees bidding summer a charming goodbye."

In 1943, with World War II still going on, winter activities and the host/hostess program were suspended at the Lodge. Members could still use the outdoor picnic area and grounds.

Word came that Adrienne Stiles arrived safely in the Middle East (without a specific location mentioned), while Ensign Ellis Persing Jr. had to forego leave due to wartime conditions.

A Christmas program and tea was held at the Lodge on December 12, 1943. Included in the evening were the Curtain Pullers from the Cleveland Playhouse, who provided Christmas pantomimes and carols. .

In the February Bulletin of 1944, it was announced that the Science Club had become an affiliating member of the Cleveland Garden Center (Now the Botanical Garden), with Miss Adele Gaede as the Club's representative on the Garden Center Committee.

On February 11, 1944, the Club visited the Western Reserve Historical Society Museum shortly after its move to University Circle from Euclid Avenue. On February 11, 1944, the Western Reserve Historical Society museum stayed open after normal hours for Science Club members and guests.

On March 17, 1944, the Club's monthly meeting was held at Cleveland College—of Western Reserve University.[50] The speaker was Mr. Stanley Morgan of Bedford's Ben Venue Laboratories. Penicillin was still so new and of such military importance that the program's content had to be approved by Washington.

On April 5, 1944, the Cleveland Conservation Forum held a meeting at the Hotel Carter. It was open to the public. The feature speaker was Dr. Hugh Bennett, Chief of the US Soil Conservation Service.

Fifty Club members attended the May, 1944, bird walk and breakfast that followed. The group sighted thirty-eight different birds.

What You Get For Your Three Dollar Dues was a three page, 8½" by 11" list describing different Lodge features, Club activities, and member benefits. It was again included with the May, 1944 Bulletin.

An exhibit of wood specimens was mounted in the museum, and attracted significant attention in the summer of 1944. It included a collection of seventy-five to one hundred wood specimens of Ohio trees. It told tree and wood history, including that of the American chestnut from which the Lodge was built. Pictures of forests around the state were displayed. Also included were samples of hickory nuts, walnuts, and chestnuts.

In November of 1944 a new Spanish Section was inaugurated so those who spoke some Spanish could meet with others and practice that tongue, "increasing one's vocabulary, and to perfect pronunciation."

At the 1944 NEOTA Meeting, the Science Club's luncheon featured three afternoon speakers:

Two movies were shown: *Airplane Changes the World Map* and *Silent War*.

Lt. Col. Wittee spoke on, "Current Problems of Local Ordnance."

Dr, H. N. Wheeler spoke again on, "Forestry in Relation to War"

In February of 1945, the Bulletin commended the Club's officers who had been able to offer programs comparable to the pre-war days and keep the Lodge open during summers and on weekends during the spring and fall. In the 1945 report to the Park Board, the Club stated, "Since it would not be in keeping with the gas rationing plan to encourage members to drive twenty-five to fifty miles to South Chagrin in order to keep in operation a full program at the Lodge, we limited activities to conform to war time regulations." Despite this consideration, the trail was maintained and the Lodge was kept open for the public.

A series of spring, summer, and fall lectures was presented by the Science Club in conjunction with Cleveland Metroparks in 1945. Open to the public, and held on Sundays in the Sulphur Springs area, this series of over sixteen presentations was "intended to foster feelings of (nature) appreciation."

A presentation on Families of Stars was made to the Club on March 23, 1945, at the Case Warner and Swasey observatory in Cleveland Heights by Dr. Nassau.

In 1945, a booklet was created listing all the plants and trees in the vicinity of the Lodge. The common name, scientific name, and a short description was provided. This was distributed to all members.

In its 1945 report to the Park Board, the Club pointed out that the host/hostess program was having positive impact. Club members answered many questions about plant and animal life of the region to numerous daily visitors, directing the public to areas of special interest. This was making a positive impact on public opinion regarding the out of doors, and the opportunities offered by Cleveland Metroparks. The value of the Lodge museum was highlighted as a benefit to the public by providing expanded interpretation of commonly observed scientific phenomena.

In 1945, representatives of the State Park of Michigan visited the Lodge to study the cooperation between the Science Club and Cleveland Metroparks. They then planned to use the Club's plans for procedures and maintenance as a guide in Michigan.

Letters from other states were also received requesting details of the Science Club's interface with the Park District and of the program and the cooperation.

The report to the Park Board in 1945 pointed out that most hosts and hostesses had a considerable natural science background, and therefore could answer the hundreds of questions asked by the public, and could direct people to places of special interest in the South Chagrin Reservation.

In 1945, development of a demonstration herb garden was planned.

A Cleveland Conservation Forum luncheon meeting, open to the public, was held at the Hotel Carter on Wednesday, April 5, 1945. Tickets were one dollar and fifty cents.

The afternoon meeting from two thirty to four thirty, and was open without charge. Featured speakers were Dr. Hugh Bennett, Chief of the US Soil Conservation Services, Louis Bromfield (nationally known conservation farmer), Dr. Jonathan Forman, Editor of the Ohio State Medical Journal, and Gllie E. Fink of the State Department of Education.

Fifty members attended the May bird walk in 1945. The Bulletin reported that "it was a beautiful day and they could have sung 'Oh What A Beautiful Morning' but they had to be quiet and look for birds." Thirty-eight birds were seen and identified.

In 1945, the annual summer picnic and field day was cancelled due to WWII, but the Lodge was open all summer with hostesses ready to inform.

It was estimated that five thousand persons visited the Lodge in 1945, while at least ten thousand benefited from the Club's activities such as the nature trail and bulletin boards. (The Lodge visitor number was estimated because some visitors neglected to sign the guest register.)

A special flyer was published during 1945 listing in the most common plants, trees, and shrubs of the South Chagrin Reservation in simple language with both scientific and common names, plus interesting facts about each species. This was a guide for going over the nature trail.

In June of 1945, the Bulletin announced "the most thrilling news the Bulletin has ever carried." It was delighted to announce that the Park Policeman had been feeding five deer this past winter. "Two does have become so tame that they come up on the Lodge grounds and can be seen from the building." (What a difference six decades makes. Now, deer are almost everywhere—in the park and in the surrounding wooded communities, due primarily to a loss of habitat, plus a lack of predators. We need a wolf pack!)

On Sunday, July 22, 1945, Mr. Shuman, Superintendent of Cuyahoga County Schools, made a presentation on rocks that anyone could understand. It was open to the public, but members who wished could bring a picnic lunch. The Club provided coffee.

From June 30 to August 25, 1946, the Club sponsored a series of nine nature-based programs at the Lodge for members and the public. The first one on June 30 was "Bringing

Grandma's Herb Garden Up To Date." The speaker discussed herbs from various categories—superstitions, culinary, historical, and medicinal.

A 172 year old maple tree that had been hit by lightening was cut down in Chardon, OH. One of the logs was sectioned at the point where holes were tapped for the sugar season. It revealed that the wood grew back, filling the holes each year, and that the tree had been tapped 157 times at this level.

On Saturday, May 18, 1946, the Club sponsored a one day trip to Mohican State Forest. It was in lieu of the pre-war overnight trip. (The Bulletin pointed out, "Still babying those tires.") During this trip, a tour was conducted by Mr. Robert Paton, Associate Forester.

There was a gathering at the Lodge on Sunday, October 15, 1946, to celebrate the War's ending.

On February 10, 1947, an Eastman Kodak Company representative gave a presentation on, "Making Pictures People Like." This was followed by a screening of the famous Kodak film titled "Cavalcade of Color." The audience expected was so large the program was held in Higbee's 10th floor lounge.

In 1947, the annual sugar bush trip was a busy day:

2:00 p.m.—Leave the Lodge for the sugar bush trip (to a local bush)

5:00 p.m.—A bring your own supper at the Lodge. The Club will provide coffee and a maple sugar stir for thirty-five cents.

6:30 p.m.—A motion picture was shown on "Cleveland's Four Seasons in the Metropolitan Parks."

8:00 p.m.—Folk Dancing

On May 17, 1947, the Club sponsored a joint meeting with the Regional Council of Science Teachers:

3:30 p.m.—A hike over the Club's nature trail

6:00 p.m.—A social hour and "bring your own" supper around the 4-sided fireplace

7:30 p.m.—A program by Mr. C.C. Andrus, head of the Weather Bureau, in the amphitheater. (Guess it didn't rain!)

On May 24, 1947, the Club held a birthday party for the tenth anniversary of the building of Look About Lodge! A full course turkey dinner was provided by a ladies group from Solon for $1.85. A program on the Club's history was presented by past-president Bertine Maloney. The dinner was named "Ellis Persing Day." In June of 1947, the Lodge museum displayed an excellent exhibit on conservation from Professor Persing's Cleveland College class.

In July of 1947, the Club planted its own herb garden "just like Grandma's" just outside the kitchen window, with all herbs labeled. A Chart of Medicinal Plants was prepared to compliment the herb garden.

The 1948 Annual Dinner was held at the College Club on February 7. The speaker was Major Dennis Glen Cooper, who described Isle Royale National Park in Lake Superior as "one of the last bits of real wilderness left east of the Mississippi," which was designated a national park on August 27, 1947.

A flyer was made for bulletin boards and other spots announcing the educational programs provided for the public by the Club. These included:

Labeled Wild Flower Trail—The Cleveland Natural Science Club maintained the trail in South Chagrin Reservation by labeling plants and trees throughout the summer from April through November, including changing labels as the wildflowers change. They also mark the trail in winter from November to April.

Sunday Morning Bird Walks—Each Sunday morning in May, at 7:15 a.m., walks are conducted from the beginning of the Sulphur Springs nature trail.

Outdoor Walks and Talks on wildflowers and trees are conducted each Sunday in May at four o'clock in the afternoon, field trips are conducted, and talks given by Club members.

During the summer of 1947, more that one hundred adult and juvenile science books were added to the Club's library.

At the December, 1947 business meeting, members approved a plan to pay for a full-time naturalist at the Lodge.

The annual Washington's Birthday party was held on February 21, 1948. The day started off with a winter hike over the trail. "There may not be any cherry trees to examine, but there will be many other trees that will challenge your ability to identify trees in winter dress.

"Be sure to bring your supper and table service, but don't bother with desert [sic] unless you don't like cherry pie. The committee will provide cherry pie and coffee for thirty five

cents." After supper a film was shown on interesting facts about Cleveland, followed by a period of games and simple folk dances.

The Annual Bird Walk was held on May 2, 1948 at 7:00 AM, followed by breakfast at the Lodge for sixty-five cents.

In May of 1948, the Club retained a fill-time naturalist for the Lodge during the summer months. The one chosen was C.W. Collins, a Cleveland Board of Education teacher. He was on duty daily in July and August in the afternoons and evenings except Mondays. He was assisted by students from the Cleveland School System.

The naturalist's program included:

- Expanded Exhibits in the Museum, beyond the resident ones, which included rocks and minerals, arrowheads, insects, and wildflowers.
- Courses and Demonstrations designed for teachers and youth group leaders.

- A Children's Program on Fridays, included nature walks and talks for groups such as Boy Scouts, Girl Scouts, Cubs, Bluebirds, Vacation Schools, and the like.
- Programs for the General Public were provided on Wednesdays, with topics of general interest. They were held at the South Chagrin Shelter House.
- Showing films to the public at the shelter house, with attendance ranging from seventy-five to one hundred and seventy five per night.

The Science Club's Field Day was resumed on July 10, 1948, beginning with a field trip starting from the Lodge at three o'clock in the afternoon. Events were scheduled on the terrace (in front of the Lodge) from four o'clock to five o'clock. Members brought their own picnic suppers to eat at five thirty

around the outdoor fireplace. The director of the Cleveland Museum of Natural History then gave a presentation on the "Indians of North America" (probably in the amphitheatre).

Again in 1948, the Club labeled wild flowers, trees, and shrubs along the South Chagrin Nature Trail. The committee of ten members (including Mr. Ralph Kneale) was chaired by Ethel Young. Ralph Kneale prepared and printed a list of edible wild plants.

In 1948, members (and the public) were invited to visit the Club's herb garden, with over thirty varieties of carefully labeled herbs in two beds west of the terrace. There was also an exhibit inside the Lodge. Six varieties of thyme were appropriately planted as a border around the sundial.

"The Culinary Garden contained such aromatic and flavorsome plants as angelica, tarragon, burnet, marjoram, basil, and rosemary, not to mention the better-known parsley, sage, and chives. The pleasant aromas from the Fragrant Garden advertise the presence of English lavender, rose geranium, rue, costmary, bergamot, santolina, heliotrope, and the tantalizing mints."

The August Bulletin listed several hints for housewives on using herbs, and two books on herbs were recommended. Hints to the housewife included:

- Chopped tarragon leaves combined with a little parsley add a delightful touch to a salad.
- Take two or three spearmint leaves and cook them with green peas and serve them with chopped beef patties.
- Fry fresh or dried sage leaves with sausages, or eat the leaves fried in butter like potato chips for a new taste thrill.

On the evening of August 21, 1948, the Club naturalist gave a presentation to members at seven o'clock in the evening. Of course, there was a bring-your-own-picnic supper at five thirty and then square dancing at eight o'clock.

The 1948 return trip to Cook Forest was on October 23 and 24, with forty-five members participating. These overnight trips had been suspended during the World War II years, due to gas rationing and tire scarcity. In 1948, rooms were $6.25 to $7.50.

In 1948, the Club again sponsored a luncheon and afternoon meeting on October 29 during the NEOTA convention. Speakers included Harold E. Wallen of the Cleveland Museum of Natural History on "Using the out-of-doors." There were also several reports on the highly successful school garden program of the Greater Cleveland School System. A movie was shown titled, *Children Grow In Gardens*.

During 1948 and 1949, the Club's naturalist recruited some fifty high school students recommended by their teachers as having good qualifications in the natural sciences. These students worked as naturalist aides during afternoon and evening naturalist programs. This gave these students experience in nature interpretation.

It was pointed out that this student aid program, done in cooperation with the Cleveland School System, gave the students an exceptional chance to become familiar with the trees, wild flowers, birds, and insects of the area, and to develop leadership in interpreting the area to park visitors. The young people had helped the naturalist in making displays for visitors at the Lodge, and marking trails with a greater variety of plants,

South Chagrin Shelter House

rocks, and trees. The students also served as guides to small groups of park visitors.

In the 1948-1949 report to the Park Board, it was stated that with the war over at least seventy-five thousand visitors had followed the nature trail, and that twelve thousand members and visitors enjoyed the Lodge facilities and programs.

A new arboretum was established on Arbor Drive in 1949. It was started with twenty-five species of trees and shrubs, all labeled, and it was open to the public. The plan was to add new species each year. On April 23, 1949, a tree planting day was held to plant trees in the vicinity of the Lodge. The tree planting day was also used to establish another arboretum by planting some two hundred evergreens near River and Miles Roads.

In the summer of 1949, the east porch became a zoo of local animals. Animals such as mice, snakes, alligators, and insects were displayed in cages, and attracted considerable attention.

This exhibit elicited many questions, plus exploration for these and other animals, such as skunks and woodchucks in the vicinity of the Lodge.

The herb garden was expanded in 1949 to include examples of medicinal herbs. This attracted much attention.

A New Educational Series of family supper programs was also started during 1949 and was very successful, drawing between fifty and one hundred fifty per night.

Bulletin No. 52 was "Rules and Regulations for Use of the Lodge by Members." There were sixteen of them. (No mention of what the other fifty-one bulletins contained.)

It was announced in 1950 that the CNSC Officers and Executive Committee had been busy making resolutions. They had pledged to emphasize broader programs in all departments, achieve greater member participation in all Club activities, and ensure continual extension of activities and services into additional allied fields of study.

It was announced in the Bulletin of February, 1950, that the Fish and Wildlife Service had pointed out that a number of snowy owls had come to Washington, DC. Normally an Arctic bird, the owls were welcome because their diet included starlings. (Apparently, there were too many starlings in our nation's capital.)

On March 4, 1950 the new Couples Section was initiated. The function of this new educational and social group was to "help the seventy-five couples on the Club membership list to become better acquainted both with each other and with the Club's programs. In this way, another service group became available to promote the general programs of the Club."

Tree Planting Day was held at the Arboretum on April 22, 1950. It was followed by Supper at the Lodge, plus a movie.

A series of courses, two to four weeks long, was offered in 1950 to the public by the Club on Birds, Trees, Photography, and Wildflowers.

At the twenty-seventh annual dinner on May 26, 1951, the focus was on the new telescope. Professor Ellis C. Persing opened the program by covering, "How the Telescope Was Built." (This must have been at least the third telescope the Club had assembled.) Also included in the program was "Presentation of" and "Acceptance of" the new telescope.

The South Chagrin Naturalist Program was a series of Thursday night programs at the South Chagrin Shelter House and was carried out by the Club during July and August of

1952, 1953, and 1954. This attracted an average attendance of seventy-five from nearby communities, as well as Boy Scouts, Cub Scouts, and other groups.

Guidebooks and checklists were made available in the 1950s for members and the general public. Updated from 1945, the checklist of trees and shrubs was prepared by Ellis C. Persing and printed by Ralph Kneale as a public service. This checklist was designed to help people note trees and shrubs of the habitat as they explore Ohio.

During the early 1950s, a number of species of plants and shrubs disappeared from the trail. To bring these native species back, the Club worked with nurserymen dealing in wild plants.

A nesting and sighting record of birds in the Cleveland region was published each year by the Kirtland Bird Club and the Cleveland Museum of Natural History. Dr. Arthur B. Williams was a guiding force for the calendar. One of the editors was Harold E. Wallin. A number of Science Club members contributed to the calendar. In 1951, a total of thirty-two people contributed sightings. A sample entry from two Science Club members for June, July, and August of 1951 follows:

"Cliff Swallows: Only three colonies were reported during 1951, two within our region, and one just outside at Huntsburg. Adele Gaede reports that three nests in which young were raised were located on Fullerton Road near Cedar Road. At the home of Mrs. Ralph Kneale on Caves Road, Chesterland, three pairs were building on the south side of an old barn on June 27. By July 2, there were eight pairs building nests. On July 13, Mrs. Kneale reported the nests destroyed by English sparrows and that the swallows had left the area.

"In July at Huntsburg, sixteen nests were built on a (freshly painted) barn under the eves. Several nests containing young dropped off after a heavy rain, and the parents immediately began building new nests. The young were raised successfully."

In 1962, a star-shaped herb garden was planned and planted by Harrison Collister and his committee on the west lawn of the Lodge near the picnic area. This was the source for herbs sold at the fall herb fair. In 1997, the garden was restored.

Bee hives were placed on the south upper porch in 1963. The hives were a nature study project, and the honey was sold at the Herb and Craft Fair.

By 1973, due to changes in membership, the Lodge could only be kept open in July and August from three to five o'clock in the afternoon on Sundays.

In 1974, the annual dinner was held at Church of the Savior in Cleveland Hts. The program was "The Story of the Colorado River," its aesthetic, recreational, biological, and educational values. In March of 1974, the Club's monthly meeting was held at the Euclid High School. The subject was astronomy and the school's planetarium was used.

In 1974, the Club continued its sponsorship of the spring bird walks in South Chagrin. The walks began at seven thirty in the morning from the shelter house. They started on April 21 and were held for six weeks.

On April 17, 1976, Duane Ferris, Kenston school teacher and Geauga Park District naturalist, gave a presentation on taking a "second look" at any nature element. Seldom is there just one item. There is usually a second point of interest. If you look closely at a weed, you may find insects on it, or animals nearby, or additional flowers associated with it.

Star shaped herb garden

On October 1, 1977, member Harvey Bicknell led a caravan through the Emerald Necklace. Starting at South Chagrin, it caravanned through Bedford, Brecksville, Hinkley, Wallace Lake, Cedar Point, and to the Rocky River Interpretive Center. The geology of the various reservations were studied. Then they stopped at Astorhurst near Tinker's Creek for dinner on the way home.

On November 19, 1977, Marshall Dietrich, Western Regional Manager of Solar Industrial Marketing for NASA, gave a slide presentation and talk on solar energy.

On March 18, 1979, the Science Club joined with the Greater Cleveland Audubon Society to caravan through the Upper Chagrin watershed—with a number of stops along the way. The event was lead by John Lillich of the Aububon Society. The groups returned to the Lodge for a picnic supper at five thirty in the evening. (John and Noreen Lillich joined the Science Club two months later.)

The Upper Chagrin River had been labeled "the cleanest river in Ohio," by the Ohio Department of Natural Resources. On this trip, the groups discussed what can be done to keep it that way. It is not known what they discussed, but subsequently the Chagrin was named a Scenic River by the State of Ohio.

The Bulletin noted that "if the weather permits, we can show the Audubon people our own beautiful little stream back of the Lodge."

Exhibits in the Lodge were tied to examples in the field in 1979, with special pointers installed to identify flowers or trees. Many examples highlighted with pointers were a distance from the trail, and would have gone unnoticed without the pointers. Another museum exhibit was of star maps and charts of data about the skies and information on how to assemble a small telescope.

A Club member provided an exhibit with color photos of fungi, mushrooms, and toad stools. He then gave a lecture and demonstration with freshly picked specimens.

In addition, the Science Club naturalist contacted Boy Scout and Girl Scout troops, plus day camp leaders and other groups for both children and adults. For these groups, the naturalist gave talks, conducted field trips, and made plans for future meetings.

On Saturday, December 1, 1979, members gathered at the Lodge for the "Hanging of the Greens." The Christmas Tea was then held on December 2.

On Saturday, December 8, 1979, Barbara Henry held a workshop on the ancient art of making apple head dolls. Members and the general public were invited. Apples were included in the three dollar fee for the workshop, but you had to "bring your own knife for peeling."

On Thursday evenings, the Club's naturalist showed special science films at the South Chagrin Shelter house. The audience ranged from seventy-five to one hundred seventy-five per night.

In addition to NEOTA luncheons, the Club hosted or provided programs to the South Euclid Garden Club, National Science Teachers' Association, Rotary Club of Chagrin Falls, new employees of the Cleveland Board of Education, plus some fifty schools, churches, and garden clubs.

Throughout 1978 and 1979, the Science Club hosted many bird, wildflower, tree, insect, and geology walks—most using the Lodge as the trailhead.

On Sunday, May 6, 1979, the Annual Bird Walk and Breakfast was held. It featured a "choice" of bird walks. Bob Furst lead a group that started at the Lodge, and Jack Rouru lead one that started at the Shelter House. Breakfast was $1.75 for adults and one dollar for children.

On three Saturdays in June, 1979, plus four Tuesdays and Thursdays, members were invited to come to the Lodge to help plant the herb garden or work on crafts. The same was scheduled for July. This activity was in preparation for the fall Herb and Craft Sale. Members were invited to bring sandwiches. Soup and salad were provided

On July 22, 1979, a guided tour of the Club's Arboretum was held, followed by a salad potluck supper. The tour was guided by Harvey Bicknell who had helped Ellis Persing Sr. plant the original arboretum.

The Club had realized that Ohio's state tree, the buckeye, had not been included in the arboretum. So, member Jack Durrell donated four small trees. They were planted near the Lodge where they could be watered and protected until they were large enough to be transplanted to the arboretum.

On February 15, 1980, the Club brought in Guy L. Denny, Assistant Chief Naturalist for the State of Ohio to speak on "Ohio Boglands, Living Relics of the Ice Age." The presentation was a multi-media event.

The program was so exceptional that the Club invited other nature clubs from Northeast Ohio to the meeting, including the Audubon, Burroughs, and Blackbrook Audubon Nature clubs. The presentation included three screens, six projectors, and 480 beautiful wildlife slides. Guy came back for a second showing on January 16, 1981, for a replay for those who missed the 1980 program due to a snow storm. And, you guessed it—there was bad weather again.

On Wednesday evenings in August and September of 1980, the Audubon Society's Jim Fulton took Science Club members on a Beaver Watch at Aurora Pond. Participants had to call for reservations, because only a few people could go each time.

In August of 1980, members were reminded that, "The only thing necessary for the triumph of evil is to have good men do nothing." Members were asked to call their congressmen to halt a pork-barrel project for the Tennessee-Tombigbee Waterway. Instead, demand that the funds be used to clean up Hazardous Waste Dump Sites. Members were reminded that political action on conservation was part of the Club's purpose.

Members were invited to join in a caravan trip to the Great Blue Heron Rookery in nearby Solon on April 12, 1980. The previous week, some thirty to thirty-five herons were sighted there circling and sitting on their large nests.

A letter was received by the Club president requesting an expansion of programs. Suggestions were mid-week programs for seniors, for nursery schools, and for day-care centers. Evening program suggestions included night hikes, photo hikes, or a history walk.

Taking Time for Recreation

Educational components were often part of recreational affairs. For example, there was a hike over the trail before the Washington's Birthday party.

There was an old, upright piano in the assembly hall. It had once belonged to President McKinley's sister-in-law. (It must have come from the first Look About Lodge.)

To relax, we would play badminton or croquet on the front (east) lawn. When it rained, members and their children would play chess, checkers, or Chinese checkers on the east porch—or in the assembly room.

When picnics were held at the shelter house in South Chagrin, there would be softball games—if enough members (and their kids) attended. There was a baseball backstop in the southeast corner of the field (near the road). We would also use the horseshoe pits that are still off the west end of the shelter house.

So, let's take a look at the Recreation activities of the Club during its tenure at the new Lodge.

A Coasting Party was held on February 4th, 1939. Members were invited to bring their own sled and meet at the Lodge between seven and seven thirty in the evening. The sledding hill was just a short walk down the hemlock trail behind the Lodge to the intersection of Sulphur Springs Drive and River Road. A full moon was promised. Soup, crackers, and coffee were served for a nominal sum.

In 1939, the anniversaries (of the Club's founding and of the first Lodge) were honored with a gala card party at the Lodge held on June 3rd.

The February, 1940, bulletin announced, "From all reports, some of us are missing healthful exercise and good times. The Dance Section offers both at seven thirty at night on February 17 and March 2. Previous experience is not a requisite."

There were quite a few picnics during the 40s. The pot-luck concept was also used for special events, like Memorial Day or Labor Day, which would often be held at the Shelter house. The ford through the Sulphur Springs creek was in use during the 1940s. It was up stream (just south of) the current footbridge. On special occasions, we would go for a short ride up the hill and back—often after breakfast—just before we returned home.

In the spring of 1942, it occurred to someone to add archery to the recreation choices at the Lodge. They then wondered why they hadn't thought of it before.

Mrs. Kneale, Card Party Chairperson, suggested in 1942 that the proceeds from the June 6 Dessert Bridge Party be used to buy a War Bond, as a way to support the war effort. Tickets were fifty-five cents for the afternoon. In addition, gifts to use as door prizes were provided by thirteen retail establishments. A one hundred dollar War Bond was purchased from the proceeds.

The November card party/fund raiser was held on November 21st in 1942, at Higbees. In November, 1943 the Bulletin noted, "More than 12 years ago the first November Card Party committee opened the doors of Higbee's Lounge to one of the Club's most essential activities. It was experimental then, but members liked that party and their guests liked it. The absentees liked what they heard about it, so the next year many of them were there with their guests.

"So, it has been ever since—indefatigable committees, and appreciative crowds. Invite your friends who enjoy games to the Higbee Lounge on Saturday, November 20, if you wish a happy solution to the problem of rationed entertaining. They do not have to be bridge players. Reserve a table for the players of pinochle or dominoes. "You will meet old friends and renew acquaintances. There will be table prizes and door prizes. There will be refreshments."

Another Fund Raising Card Party was held on November 13, 1948. (Remember, this was long before TV.) This one was also held at Higbee's Lounge and Silver Grill—a restaurant with an accompanying meeting room in a downtown Cleveland department store.

The purpose was to "Keep the Wolf from Our Door" by paying for maintenance of the Lodge. The committee apologized for having to raise the price to $1.25 (but that included tax, of course).

Pot luck dinners are an old concept that probably became more popular during the depression. Just as today, people would be assigned a dish to bring—casserole or meat and vegetable, salad or desert. The hot dishes could be warmed up (or the cooking could be finished) in the kitchen.

Some members also picnicked in the Euclid Creek Reservation (We used to call it Bluestone). There was a shelter house at the north end of the park where bird-calling contests were held each spring.

In 1947, Washington's Birthday was another busy day. It included:

2:30 p.m.—A winter field trip over the trail They went for a hike to identify trees by their bark and shape and see the winter trail labels and bulletin board. A list of what could be seen is in Appendix D.

5:45 p.m.—Bring your own supper. The Club furnished cherry pie and coffee.

7:00 p.m.—An illustrated talk by Dr. James Gray on "Our Insect Friends and Foes."

7:30 p.m.—A social hour of games and laughs.

9:00 p.m.—Folk dancing.

A Christmas Program was held annually at the Lodge. There was always entertainment and the singing of carols. In 1947, entertainment was provided by the Curtain Pullers from the Cleveland Playhouse.

In 1948, the Annual Spring Card Party was held on June 5th. The fee for desert and coffee was seventy-four cents, including a twelve cent tax.

In 1974, the Club celebrated its fiftieth anniversary with a dinner and program at the Lodge on May 18th. One hundred eight members and guests attended. Grace Marriott was president of the Science Club during this fiftieth anniversary year.

The printed program's section on "The Future," espoused, "The future belongs to the wonderful young people of today, and we hope those who carry on for the third quarter of our century [The Club's] will be as sincerely devoted to the *purpose* of our organization as those who established and loved it through the past fifty years.

"Our purpose is still '*to promote the study of our natural sciences, to cultivate an appreciation of the outdoors, to advance the conservation of our natural resources, and to protect wild animal and plant life.*

Note the rifle above the fireplace.

"Now, we place in your hands a challenge to the young and a trust to the mature, to promote legislation which will protect our environment for the benefit of future generations."

The Club also held a Fiftieth Anniversary Open House on July 21. Some sixty members and guests attended that event.

Throughout the summer and fall of 1976, members entertained small groups to which they belonged at the Lodge. These groups included Church Circles, Prayer Groups, Campfire Girls, Garden Clubs, and Senior Citizen groups. On December 5, 1976, at the Christmas Tea, the program was "Christmas in Early America," a musical program of ensemble singing, solos, duets, and audience participation. Accompaniment was multiple violins and piano.

On June 23, 1979, the Annual Spring Card Party was held. On August 18, 1979 the Club held a corn roast in the picnic area. Sweet Corn and watermelon were provided. Following supper, Bob and Ruth English, well-known nature photographers, showed some of their insect pictures. (You can't have just a picnic; you need to have something educational.)

On Thursday, November 22, 1979, a Thanksgiving feast was held at the Lodge—for members who might otherwise be alone. The turkeys were "fresh from the farm." On Thursday, November 27, 1980, a Thanksgiving feast was again held at the Lodge, Members were allowed to bring one or two guests.

Making Time for Operations

T he annual business meeting was where the business of the Club was discussed and new initiatives begun such as raising dues, expanding the board, etc. It is the only meeting held for members only. It was usually held in December.

Operational and financial affairs were necessary for administration of the Club, and were especially crucial during the depression. Lodge maintenance was handled by Club members when possible, thereby reducing the operations budget.

In November of 1940, the Cleveland Natural Science Club finally got around to registering with the State of Ohio as a "corporation not for profit." The first entry in the corporate record book is dated November 17, 1940.

So, let's take a look at the Operational activities of the Club during its occupation of the new Lodge. Highlights of such activities include the following:

In 1938-39, the request for a five dollar donation from each member to help finance the new Lodge brought in "a good response," and the building committee thanked members for their support. (Remember, this was still during the Great Depression.)

By December, 1938, The Cleveland Natural Science Club's membership totaled 250 (the year of the new Lodge's dedication). Dues were increased again by fifty cents.

In May of 1939, an article in the Bulletin reminded members that there is no eating in the assembly room. Use the outdoor fireplace picnic area or the screened east porch. "The assembly room is the Lodge's *guest room* or *sitting room*, and should always be ready for guests."

Also in May of 1939, it was announced that additional picnic tables had been added to the four-sided fireplace picnic area.

In 1939, professional sinks were installed in the darkroom and the floor was painted.

To keep the Lodge "Open To The Public" (and to members), the January Bulletin in 1940 again enticed members, *"Are there some Club members who have not had the opportunity to enjoy being hosts or hostesses at the Lodge? It is truly a beautiful spot these winter weekends and very comfortable. Mr. Persing will be glad to list the open dates. You are asked to stay only during the afternoon of Saturday and Sunday unless you wish to remain overnight."* In another issue, it pointed out that being a hostess/ host at the Lodge was a real treat. It was like having your own country estate.

In July of 1940, select male members were invited to join the Janitor Squad. (The majority of members were still women school teachers.) This was to be a group of eight or ten men who could be called upon to open the Lodge whenever necessary, which included making a fire in the (coal) furnace as well as the fireplaces. A one dollar reimbursement of expenses would be allowed for gas, etc. With a ten-person team, each member would be called upon less frequently.

On October 1, 1940 the latest additions to the Lodge were a coal and wood stove—modernized to compliment the oil stove—a coat rack in the front lobby, and copper drain pipes. These were installed due to the successes of the Annual Picnic and the August party.

On May 10, 1941, members again came to the Lodge to do spring housecleaning. The Club could afford to hire two workers to do the heavy work, but there were a host of small jobs that needed doing. There were two lists, one of *Men's* jobs and one of *Women's* jobs. (The women had seven jobs, the men had sixteen.)

The Club paid three dollars per month for a telephone in 1941, with calls to Cleveland and its near suburbs costing ten cents for five minutes. Calls that exceeded five minutes were charged long distance rates.

On October 21, 1942, Arthur Munson and Professor Persing were named Honorary Members of the Cleveland Natural Science Club for outstanding services contributed.

In an effort to comply with war-time shortages of gasoline and tires, the Lodge closed on November 14 for the winter of 1942—1943. The Bypath kept publishing to keep members informed of Club activities. Trail and grounds maintenance was also continued. The plan was to have one meeting a month in an in-town location.

An Annual Clean-up, Shine-up Day was planned for May 22, 1943, with both work and play scheduled.

On Wednesday, December 8, 1943, the Annual Business Meeting was held at the Cleveland Health Museum. This museum was housed in an old "millionaires' row" mansion on Euclid Avenue. The meeting was at 7:15 p.m., followed by a lecture with pictures and a tour of the museum at eight o'clock.

Housekeeping crew stops for lunch. (Note the snowy owl on the shelf behind tand above the table.)

The evening ended with movies appropriate for the occasion at nine o'clock.

In 1944, the business meeting was held at the Western Reserve Historical Society in University Circle. This meeting was followed by a tour of the museum.

In 1944, members were urged to mail their dues to the treasurer before April 1, when the cost of a stamp would rise to three cents.

The literature on *What You are Able to Enjoy for Your $3.50 Dues* was again distributed with the May, 1944 Bulletin.

On the Saturdays of May 12 and May 19, 1945, members came to the Lodge for spring house cleaning. It was a bring your own lunch and *try to have some fun* affair.

An outdoor drinking fountain was installed at the Lodge on November 9, 1946, a gift from Ida Henry. (Bet it had cold water!) It is still there and it still works.

In January of 1947, the number of trustees for the club was raised from four to six.

In the spring, a Lodge cleanup day was held to prepare the building for the summer season. This included cleaning and waxing.

In the fall, a maintenance day was scheduled to prepare the Lodge for winter and to make any repairs on the "To Do" list.

In August of 1948, a request for member volunteers was made to paint the Lodge. The Club's men members gave the Lodge a complete paint job. Stain and creosote was applied where needed to prevent deterioration of the building. The fences and out buildings were done as well. In addition , the windows were re-puttied. It was a cost-saving activity.

In October of 1948, it was announced that sixteen new members had joined the Club since January. (That included the Club's new naturalist.)

A Caulking Party was held on November 6, 1948. It drew twenty-six Club men and women. The objective was to prepare for winter by sealing up the cracks between the logs caused by "our friends the squirrels" and other creatures. (Why did they caulk after they painted?)

In 1948, some twenty volunteers did the Lodge cleanup, saving the expense of commercial cleaners. It was another cost-saving activity.

In December of 1948, a meeting of the membership was called to discuss solutions to the budget shortfall for 1948 of about five hundred dollars and roughly four hundred dollars projected for 1949. There was a need to increase income by 40 to 50 percent.

In 1949, dues were raised to five dollars per year for members, plus two dollars for spouses.

Members were again advised to carry their membership cards, because Cleveland Metroparks Rangers had been instructed to ask for identification of all who are on the premises.

At the 1974 annual meeting, Mr. Ralph M. Kneale was elected Trustee to fill an existing vacancy.

On May 4th and 11th of 1974, Lodge Cleanup days were again scheduled. Those who couldn't be there were asked to make a contribution to defray expenses.

In 1976, membership leveled out. Thirteen new members were accepted, bringing total membership to 172.

Attendance at the monthly meetings rose to 2,123 in 1977, which was 423 more than 1976. This was despite canceling two meetings due to bad weather. (Careful figures were kept for the annual report to the Park Board.)

By 1979, Club dues had increased to $12.50 for single members and twenty dollars for a family (and thirty dollars for a sustaining member).

In 1979, the Annual House Cleaning of the Lodge was scheduled for two Saturdays—May 5 and May 12. Maybe there weren't enough volunteers

Thanks to the fall card party in 1979, and nine corporate supporters of the event, the annual 1980 spring "beauty treatment" of the Lodge could be paid for and done by professionals.

On October 13, 1979, the Club held a Herb and Craft fair for the public at the Lodge. They sold herbs, crafts, baked goods, and white elephant items to raise funds. Items for sale in the "English Kitchen" included jams, jellies, and houseplants. Barbecued hot dogs and coffee were sold as refreshments. Girl Scouts helped by running errands during the sale, and the men helped with car parking.

In 1979, over one hundred and fifty wreaths were made by Jean Mossburger and sold at the Club's Fair. Mickie Hecker made all the dried arrangements, and many members participated in the creation of crafts sold at the fair. Then, they rented booths at the Orange and Solon craft fairs and sold more.

This was the second such Fair organized by Club president Julia Jewell. The first had been a year earlier. The function, of course, was to make money to maintain the Lodge.

.In January of 1980, outgoing president Julia Jewell thanked all the members for their support during the past year, and quoted an Army officer who once said, "It ain't the individual, or army as a whole, but the everlasting teamwork of every blooming Soul.."

In 1980, a swarm of bats decided the Lodge was a good home. Their high-pitched screams set off the security alarm, causing Cleveland Metroparks Rangers to respond and causing the Club president to come to the Lodge and shut off the alarm. This prompted the addition of wire mesh screens over both chimneys.

On Saturday, October 11, 1980, Cleveland Metroparks asked for volunteers to help keep Cleveland's "jewel of nature" clean by picking up litter. The Science Club, of course, participated.

Oakum is the fiber that is wedged between the logs of a log building to make it weatherproof. It had come loose in places and needed to be poked back. On Saturday, October 18, 1980 they made a party of it. The job required initially two people—one outside and one inside. For the higher logs, two more people were required to hold the ladders—inside and out.

In 1993, with membership down to one hundred, the annual housecleaning was started on Saturday, May 5th. The next Saturday, the 12th, was scheduled as a day to "finish housecleaning." This service work was combined with good fun and fellowship.

A Management Change:

Look About Lodge operation and maintenance was transferred to Cleveland Metroparks in 1993, with a continuing use agreement given to the Cleveland Natural Science Club for their monthly meetings.

This enabled major maintenance improvements to the building and opened the natural beauty and inspiring atmosphere of the Lodge to significantly more people. So, operation of Look About Lodge, built and paid for by Science Club members, was given over for the use of its owner, Cleveland Metroparks.

In 1993, Dr. Robert D. Hinkle, Chief Naturalist of Cleveland Metroparks, wrote: "For over fifty years, members of the Cleveland Natural Science Club have dedicated themselves to the enhancement of learning about the outdoors. Their series of monthly seminars has brought many of the region's best naturalists and field biologists to the Lodge to share their knowledge with members and guests. Cleveland Metroparks is proud to have accepted the responsibility of restoring Look About Lodge, a magnificent gift from past generations. Want to walk up and down a Cleveland Metroparks nature trail virtually unchanged since 1938? You can find this, and many other new program directions, at Look About Lodge in South Chagrin Reservation. Thoreau once said that he had 'gone to the woods, to live more deliberately.' At South Chagrin Reservation, it is time to return to the woods, back to the heritage, which gave this nation its uniqueness of character. Come with us and 'live deliberately' as you discover a new initiative in outdoor education programming excellence in the wonderful gift from the past, Look About Lodge."

Today, the Cleveland Natural Science Club meets at the Lodge January through November on the third Saturday of each month. It sponsors a program on a nature subject at 7:30 p.m. that is open to the public. For more information, call 440-247-7075. In December, a Christmas Tea is held for members and their guests.

The Club's Founder

"Joy in the universe, and keen curiosity about it all—that has been my religion."

—*John Burroughs*

Professor Ellis C. Persing attended Columbia University and ultimately became a professor in Western Reserve University's School of Education. I remember him as having a happy and positive personality—truly joyous and keenly curious!

Born November 1885, he was the son of Henry Persing and Naomi Patterson. Ellis was schooled in Snydertown, in eastern Pennsylvania. Early in his career, he was principal and manual training teacher in Cooperstown, North Dakota.

In 1919, Ellis Persing was hired by Western Reserve University as a professor. His area of expertise was the natural sciences. In the early 1920s, a course in natural science was first offered by the Education College. In fact, Professor Persing introduced the concept of teaching the natural sciences as an interesting subject for the elementary grades.

Ellis Persing published a number of works. Beginning in 1928, he authored a series of six books for elementary school level titled *Elementary Science by Grades: A Nature Study and Science Reader*, with color illustrations.[51] He then chaired a committee of Cleveland Teachers, which authored *A Manual For General Sciences in the Ninth Grade*. The fifteen page manual was priced at twenty-five cents.

He also wrote, *Pupils' and Teachers' Interpretation of Common Scientific Phenomena*. His eleven page article on, *Constructing the Elementary-Science Course in Cleveland*, appeared in *The Elementary School Journal* of April, 1929. In 1953, at the age of sixty-eight, he authored a book on insect collecting as a hobby.

It was the nineteen students in his first class of natural science for elementary grades that formed the Cleveland Nature Club, which then became the Cleveland Natural Science Club

A long time resident of Shaker Heights, Ellis Persing, passed away in 1956 at age seventy-one in Snydertown, Northumberland County, Pennsylvania. Services were held at Epworth-Euclid Methodist Church, with interment in Lake View Cemetery—also the final resting place and monument of President James A. Garfield.

The key to the success of the Cleveland Natural Science Club, and the Look About Lodges, during the Club's first 60 years was the comprehensive and expanding education program provided to the public. This program was ultimately taken over and further expanded by the Cleveland Metroparks using full-time naturalists.

Real Inspiration

✦ External Events ⚑ Naturalist and nature events ☞ Cleveland Metroparks events ➢ Cleveland Natural Science Club and Look About Lodge events

Ellis Persing provided both the inspiration and leadership that enabled the Cleveland Natural Science Club—and Look About Lodge. As one Club member phrased it in 1940, "This Club, this Lodge, the trail, and everything for which they stand are a monument to the untiring, persevering pursuit of an ideal by Mr. Persing for which we are all grateful."

Grace Marriott was president of the Science Club during its fiftieth anniversary year. Her comments in 1974 on Arthur Munson, Ellis Persing, and Ed Doller included, "The good men do lives after them! All the good the past hath had remains to make our own time glad." She completed her remarks by pointing out, "We, you and I, are the recipients of that good. We are the beneficiaries and are very grateful to all those dedicated people who gave so much of themselves to make our own time glad."

✦ External Events ⚒ Naturalist and nature events ☞ Cleveland Metroparks events ➤ Cleveland Natural Science Club and Look About Lodge events

lodge spirit 141

A Timeline of Nature Appreciation That Lead To Cleveland Metroparks and The Cleveland Natural Science Club and Look About Lodge

As stated in Chapter 1, Look About Lodge became an entity due to a series of natural science and conservation influences and events. The following timeline is provided to help put those influences and events into context. Dates of external events have also been added to aid your perspective:

The Early Years

🌲 May 23, 1699: John Bartram is born in Pennsylvania.

✦ 1776: The United States declared its independence.

🌲 1777: John Bartram dies at age seventy-eight.

🌲 1785: John Audubon is born in Santa Domingo.

✦ 1792—1802: French Revolutionary Wars.

✦ April 11, 1803—The Louisiana Purchase was made from France.

✦ 1803—1806: President Thomas Jefferson sent Lewis & Clark on their expedition to explore the land obtained through the Louisiana Purchase.

✦ 1803—1815: Napoleonic Wars.

✦ 1812—1815: War of 1812 between United States and England.

🌲 1838: John Muir is born in Dunbar, Scotland.

🌲 July 4, 1845: Henry David Thoreau moves to Walden Pond.

🌲 1847: George Perkins Marsh gave a speech to the Agricultural Society of Rutland County VT on the

---

✦ External Events 🌲 Naturalist and nature events ☞ Cleveland Metroparks events ➤ Cleveland Natural Science Club and Look About Lodge events

destructive impact of human activity on the land, especially deforestation.

🔥 April 3, 1837: John Burroughs was born in Roxbury, New York.

✦ 1847: The California Gold Rush began.

🔥 January 27, 1851: John Audubon dies at age sixty-six.

🔥 1852: The Hot Springs Reservation in Arkansas was set aside by the Federal government because of the medicinal qualities believed to be possessed by its waters. The reservation did not became a national park, however, until 1921.

🔥 1860: Ernest Thompson (Ernest Thompson Seton) is born in Durham, England.

✦ April 12, 1861: The Civil War begins with shots fired on Fort Sumter.

🔥 May 6, 1862: Henry David Thoreau dies.

🔥 1864: Henry David Thoreau's book titled, *The Maine Woods* is published. The book advocated the establishment of national preserves of virgin forest.

🔥 1864: George Perkins Marsh publishes, *Man and Nature or The Earth As Modified By Human Action.*

🔥 1864: Yosemite first becomes a park when the US Congress passed legislation giving Yosemite Valley to the state of California for use as parkland.

✦ 1864: America's first zoo was established in Philadelphia.

✦ April 9, 1865: The Civil War ends when General Lee surrenders to General Grant.

🔥 1866: The word *ecology* was first used by a German biologist named Ernst Haeckel.

🔥 1869: John Muir moves into the Yosemite Valley.

🔥 September 19, 1870: The Washarn-Langford-Doane Expedition sets out to investigate the natural wonders in the Yellowstone area.

🔥 December 18, 1871: The National Park Act was presented to the US House of Representatives.

🔥 March 1, 1872: The first National Park was established when Congress passed and President Ulysses S. Grant signed the National Parks Act, allowing Yellowstone to be set aside as a national park.

🔥 1886: The Audubon Society was formed—some 35 years after its namesake's death.

🔥 October 1, 1890: Yosemite, which had been set aside as a California State Park, became a National Park, along with the General Grant and Sequoia National Parks.

✦ External Events 🔥 Naturalist and nature events ☞ Cleveland Metroparks events ➤ Cleveland Natural Science Club and Look About Lodge events

1891: The Forest Reserve Act was passed by the US Congress, allowing forest set-asides. This was the start of our national forest system which is unique in the world.

June 4, 1892: The Sierra Club was founded by John Muir and Century Magazine publisher Robert Underwood Johnson. John Muir became the club's first president.

1893: Ernest Thompson Seton travels to New Mexico to hunt a wolf known as Lobo.

August 18, 1896: The Alaska gold rush was started when a salmon fisherman found nuggets in a creek bed.

1898: Gilford Pinchot was appointed Chief, Division of Forestry, US Department of Agriculture. This began the era of forestry where clear cutting was to be abandoned.

1901: Theodore Roosevelt became President of the United States.

1901: The first Sierra Club outing was made to Tuolomne Meadows, which lies some 2000 feet above the Yosemite Valley floor.

1903: John Muir takes President Theodore Roosevelt on a tour of the "exquisite Yosemite."

1905: William Stitchcomb first proposes a metropolitan park system that would encircle Greater Cleveland like a necklace.

June 8, 1906: The Antiquities Act gives President Theodore Roosevelt[53] authority "to declare by public proclamation historic landmarks, structures, and other objects of scientific interest."

1909: William Stitchcomb again proposes a metropolitan park system for Cleveland.

1910: The Lakeview Gusher began spewing crude oil into the air of the San Joaquin Valley in California. The gusher released 125,000 barrels per day. About half was captured while the remainder flowed into California's rivers and streams.

Cleveland's Nature Preservation Tradition Begins

1912: Cleveland forms a Park Board.

1913: The US Congress authorized the damming of the Hetch Hetchy Valley in Yosemite National Park to provide water for San Francisco and the surrounding area.

August 1, 1914: Official outbreak of World War I. Germany declares war on Russia.

December 24, 1914: John Muir, the mountain man, dies at age seventy-six.

✦ External Events ♠ Naturalist and nature events ☞ Cleveland Metroparks events ➤ Cleveland Natural Science Club and Look About Lodge events

☞ 1915: Ohio law was changed to allow the Cuyahoga County Commissioners to appropriate money to the park board.

⚒ 1915: The California legislature authorized funding for the planning and building of the John Muir Trail.

⚒ 1915: Congress approved a $280,000 budget for the US Biological Survey budget, stipulating that $125,000 of the budget be used to destroy wolves, coyotes, and any other animals considered to be detrimental to agriculture, meaning primarily livestock farming. Under the wolf extermination program, many trappers were employed full time in this endeavor.

☞ 1916: William Stinchcomb, who had been elected Cuyahoga County engineer, first received funds to develop the "Cuyahoga County Park and Boulevard System."

⚒ 1916: The National Park Service was established to manage the growing National Park System.

✦ April, 1917: US enters WWI by declaring war on Germany.

☞ July 23, 1917: Cleveland Metroparks is the first Park District established in Ohio, created to provide open space for the people of Greater Cleveland, as well as to conserve and preserve the natural valleys of the area.

✦ November 11, 1918: Armistice Day declared—WWI fighting ceases at eleven in the morning.

➢ Early 1920s: Professor Ellis C. Persing of Western Reserve University (Cleveland, Ohio) met outside of the classroom with students from his Education College course on teaching the natural sciences to "further their discussions."

⚒ March 29, 1921: John Burroughs dies on a train in Kingsville, Ohio while returning from California.

➢ May 21, 1924: First entry made in the corporate record book of "The Cleveland Nature Club." There were nineteen charter members, plus Professor Persing. All but Prof. Persing were alumni of Western Reserve University's Education College. This was the group who, as students, had been meeting with Professor Persing outside of the classroom to discuss the natural sciences.

➢ September 26, 1925: The Nature Club's name was changed to, "The Cleveland Natural Science Club."

⚒ 1926: The last two wolves in Yellowstone were killed.

➢ February 7, 1928: The first Annual Dinner of The Cleveland Natural Science Club was held.

☞ 1928: Nature Trails for Cleveland Metroparks were laid out and labeled by The Cleveland Museum of Natural History.

✦ External Events ⚒ Naturalist and nature events ☞ Cleveland Metroparks events ➢ Cleveland Natural Science Club and Look About Lodge events

✦ October 29, 1929: Stock Market crash in America, and the start of the Great Depression..

⚞ 1930: Ernest Thompson Seton envisions the idea for an Academy of Outdoor Life, shortly after he moved to Santa Fe, New Mexico.

☞ 1930: The Cleveland Museum of Natural History gave Dr. Arthur B. Williams the *special assignment* of naturalist for the Cleveland Metropolitan Park Board[54].

➤ May 10, 1930: The first nature trail opened in Bedford Glens—established by the Cleveland Natural Science Club.

The Move to a Natural Location

➤ April, 1931: The first Cleveland Natural Science Club clubhouse was established when use of the old Winslow farmhouse in Bentleyville was obtained by the Cleveland Natural Science Club. The new "clubhouse" was named "Look About Lodge"[55].

➤ June 6, 1931: The Old Winslow House Look About Lodge was accepted from the Cleveland Metropolitan Park Board.

☞ July 4, 1931: The first trailside museum was established in the North Chagrin Reservation of Cleveland Metroparks.

⚞ 1931: The Holden Arboretum is established in Lake County, protecting over three thousand acres from development. It was sanctioned by the Cuyahoga County Court of Common Pleas. Trees were planted, collections established, and programs begun.

✦ 1931 to 1934: Bonnie and Clyde went on their robbery spree.

✦ 1933: Franklin Delano Roosevelt becomes president.

➤ 1935: Professor Ellis Persing initiated the effort to build a new Look About Lodge.

⚞ 1935: The Wilderness Society was founded in response to, "an emergency in conservation which requires no delay in the craze to build all the highways possible everywhere …."

➤ June 8, 1935: An Alaskan Totem Pole was presented to the Science Club for its new Lodge. Ellis Persing purchased the totem after his Science Club Travel Section trip to Alaska, The cost was $60.00, plus $7.50 for shipping. The purchase was arranged by the Canadian Pacific Railway.

➤ October 21, 1936: Arthur Munson and Ellis Persing choose the location for the new Look About Lodge. The foundation was dug soon after.

➤ 1937: The new Look About Lodge was built from 309 American chestnut logs, totaling five thousand linear feet.

✦ External Events ⚞ Naturalist and nature events ☞ Cleveland Metroparks events ➤ Cleveland Natural Science Club and Look About Lodge events

➤ June 5, 1938: The new Look About Lodge was dedicated, and formally opened for use by members and guests—it was opened to the public on June 23.

☞ December, 1938: Cleveland Metroparks had grown to nearly eleven thousand acres in six reservations, with between four and five million people visiting the parks annually.

✦ September 1st 1939: Germany invaded Poland and World War II began.

➤ December 9, 1940: The Science Club was incorporated as an "Ohio Corporation Not For Profit."

✦ December 7, 1941: Japan invades Pearl Harbor in Hawaii, drawing the United States into World War II. This effectively ends the Great Depression.

☞ Park Education Was Growing: By the summer of 1942, Cleveland Metroparks Outdoor Education Division had seven well-qualified associates. There were three well-equipped trailside museums plus nature trails, guided trips through the Parks District, and regularly scheduled lectures.

➤ July, 1943: (during WWII) Ensign Ellis Persing Jr. had to forego a leave due to wartime conditions.

✦ May 8, 1945: VE Day—Victory in Europe.

✦ September 2, 1945: VJ Day—Formal surrender by Japan, ending WWII.

⚒ 1946: Ernest Thompson Seton dies at his castle in New Mexico on October 23 at the age of eighty-six.

✦ October, 1948: An atmospheric inversion occurred in Donora, Pennsylvania at the US Steel Zinc Works that caused twenty deaths and made many others sick. The public outcry eventually lead to the Air Pollution Control Air Act of 1955, followed by the Clean Air Act of 1970.

➤ 1952: The CNSC affiliates with the Nature Conservancy, a national organization for the protection and use of our natural resources.

☞ 1954: Education became a priority for Cleveland Metroparks when they established a new department of education and named Harold E. Wallin as park naturalist.

➤ 1957: The Persing Memorial Garden was established.

➤ September 21, 1963: The 25th anniversary of the new Look About Lodge dedication was celebrated.

☞ 1964: A year-round schedule was begun by Cleveland Metroparks when a full-time naturalist was hired for the North Chagrin Reservation, and the trailside museum was kept open all year long. Three years later, the Rocky River Reservation achieved the same status with a naturalist and year-round operation.

✦ External Events   ⚒ Naturalist and nature events   ☞ Cleveland Metroparks events   ➤ Cleveland Natural Science Club and Look About Lodge events

☞ 1967: Natural science education and interpretation—With year-round staffing, Cleveland Metroparks was serving 226 classes totaling 10,592 students. This included classes visiting the museums, and the reservation naturalists visiting school classrooms. This service continues today.

☞ October, 1975: The Zoo, Too—Cleveland Metroparks took over operation of the Cleveland Zoo. It had taken over responsibility for the over 160 acres of land and the buildings some five years earlier. Cleveland's zoo is the fifth oldest in the United States.

☞ 1984: Attendance ascends at Cleveland Metroparks, growing to 21.3 million, and in 1985 it exceeded 21.5 million. The Park's ten reservations encompassed over seventeen thousand acres.

☞ 1993: The End of an Era: Due to high maintenance and a changed Science Club membership, an agreement was made with Cleveland Metroparks to take over operation of Look About Lodge.

The Recent Years

Look About Lodge was entered into the National Register of Historic Places in 2007.[56] The application for this recognition included the following:

"Look About Lodge is a rustic, rectangular, two-story meeting hall in an isolated setting on Miles Road near Chagrin River Road in the Village of Bentleyville. The setting is on the northeast edge of Cleveland Metroparks two thousand-acre South Chagrin Reservation, which has many miles of foot and bridle trails winding through a variety of natural habitats.

"Bentleyville is an outer suburb of greater Cleveland in the southeast corner of Cuyahoga County. The communities of Solon, Bainbridge, Chagrin Falls, and Moreland Hills surrounding the Lodge are semi-rural, containing many large and wooded lots.

"A curved driveway leads to a sixty-car parking lot. The Lodge sits in a flat, open area surrounded by beech, maple, and hemlock trees. There is a stone walkway around the entire building. Picnic tables are available in several locations near the Lodge.

"A number of changes were made to the Lodge in recent years, including a new cedar shake roof installed in 1993. The south porch was completely removed, and replaced in 1998 using the original design and techniques, but without the gargoyles. American chestnut, of course, was no longer available, so white oak was used."

As Cleveland Metroparks took over natural science education plus Look About Lodge maintenance and occupation, the Cleveland Natural Science Club's activities and service opportunities changed substantially.

In 2009, Cleveland Metroparks' welcomed nearly 46 million visitors, with some 17,740 of them visiting Look About Lodge. Many were schoolchildren on a natural science field trip. Adult programs ranged from the natural sciences for the public and for teachers to folk music.

The Club still holds monthly meetings the third Saturday of each month with a pot-luck dinner for members (except in December). The Club provides programs at 7:30 PM on nature and conservation at each meeting. The programs are still "open to the public." For the names and phone numbers of the membership chairperson and the Club president, phone 440-247-7075.

The original members have all passed away, and the Club has lost much of its "service" stewardship. The opportunities to support the natural sciences have changed, but they are still there. The Cleveland Natural Science Club is ripe for new membership that is dedicated to nature appreciation and wants to provide support in creative ways to the Cleveland Metroparks and to Greater Clevelanders.

Postlogue

It is amazing what one creative and inspired professor was able to accomplish! The confluence of events that enabled Greater Cleveland's Look About Lodge is also amazing. Today's Lodge is a living and vibrant monument to the many creative and dedicated people who made it happen.

It can be argued that Look About Lodge takes its place among the many other rustic monuments to nature appreciation such as the Awanee in Yosemite National Park and Old Faithful Lodge in Yellowstone. Look About Lodge and the early years of the Cleveland Natural Science Club are testaments to what can be done when creative and dedicated people put their minds to it!

It has been pointed out that this narrative covers almost a century of Greater Cleveland's past. I am honored to have been in a position to compile this important part of its natural history.

Appendices

Appendix A. Cleveland Natural Science Club Charter Members

Founded/First Meeting: May 2, 1924

*Mr. Ellis C. Persing

*Miss Abby Louise Amy

Miss Bertha Burnett

Miss Pearl Dreher

*Miss Margaret Elandman

*Miss Blanche E. Hornbeck

Miss Elsie Linn

Miss Olga C. Lynn

Mrs. Lulu Marshall

Miss Eleanor J. Radcliffe

*Mr. F. P. Schweikler

Miss Lulu B. Shepard

*Miss Rose Singer

Miss Lillian Thomson

*Miss Florence Travis

Miss Bertha Wager

Miss Ellen Wager

Miss Alice W. Wicks

Miss Myra B. Wohrer

Miss Sarah Zsupnyik

*Still Active in 1938

*1938 Officers (The year the new look
About Lodge was dedicated)*

Helen G. Miller—President

Ellis C. Persing—Permanent Vice Pres.

Bertine Maloney—Second Vice Pres.

Grace Curry—Treasurer

Edna Hopp—Correspondence Sec.

Esther Leonhardt—Recording Sec.

Agnes Strothman—Bulletin Editor

Executive Committee

Mirza Aurand

J. C. Minich

Catherine MacFarlane

Warren Miller

Building Committee

Fred G. Baker

Edward W. Doller

Ellis C. Persing

Conservation Committee

F. P. Schweikher—Supervisor, Department of Elementary Nature Study and Gardening, Cleveland Heights School System

Mary Melrose—Supervisor, Elementary Science, Cleveland Schools

Vincent Peterson—Biology Department, Glenville High School

Life Member: Edna K. Wooley

Appendix B. Cleveland Natural Science Club Presidents

Ellis C. Persing 1924–25

F.P. Schweikler 1926–27

Florence G. Travis 1928–31

Helen K. Bret 1932

C.C. Steele 1933–34

Bertine Maloney 1935–36

Helen Miller 1937–38

Edward W. Doller 1939–40

Marian Kirsch 1941–42

Viola Neuman 1943–44

Fanny Lindsay 1945–46

Dorothy Warner 1947–48

John Stewart 1949–51

Ann Burgess 1952

Harold Laing 1953–54

Vincent R. Peterson 1955–56

John Stewart 1957–58

Bruce Maddux 1959–60

George Inman 1961–63

Charles Collins 1964–66

Ellis C. Persing, Jr. 1967

Howard Sample 1968

Richard W. Hoffman 1969

Marian Snider 1970–71

Harian Newell 1972

David C. Marsh 1973

John C. Langmead 1974

Grace Marriott 1975–77

Julia Jewell 1978–79

Michael D'Amato 1980

Jeanne M. Furst 1981–84

Rose Halecek 1985–86

Joan Freemantle 1/87–6/87

Jack Rouru 7/87–1991

Bill Banks 1992–93

Grover Ramsey 1994

Lynn Burt 1995–96

Roger Furmeyer 1997–98

Mary Lou Rouru 1999–01

Shirley Ashby 2002–04

Roger Furmeyer 2005

Mary Lou Rouru 2006–07

Julianne Sliwinski 2008–09

Ann Hammond 2010-11

Shirley Ashby 2012

Appendix C. Early Years' Club
Sections and Committees

Astronomy Section

Elementary Education Section

Folk Dance Section

Men's' Section

Section K (photography)

Section Q (WRU Students)

Section X (Travel Section)

Building Committee

House & Grounds Committee

Executive Committee

Hospitality Committee

Sunshine Committee

Social Committee

Conservation Committee

Trail Committee

Herb and Flower Garden Committee

Museum Committee

Arboretum Committee

Historian

Committees for special events included

Telescope Committee

Family Supper (each month)

Valentine's Day

Washington's Birthday Party

May Breakfast

Spring Card party

Fall Card Party

Halloween Party

Christmas Tea Party

In 1950, Additional Committees were Added/Updated

Arboretum

Building and Grounds

Couples

Educational Program

Finance

Publications

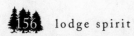

Appendix D. What You Might Have Seen On the Winter Trail Behind the Lodge—in February of 1947

Red berries on wintergreen and partridge berry

Yellow ribbon petals and last years seed pods on witch hazel

Goldenrod seed tufts

Velvety red berries in clusters on the sumac

Ground cedar fruiting bodies

Mosses and lichens growing on the same stone

Grape fern with fruiting stem

Christmas fern just over the creek

Green leaves on the hepatica

Beech drops under the beech trees

Shelf fungus on a young beech tree

Lacy green hemlock boughs

Turkey tail fungus on young growth of shrubbery

Winter birds

Blue jays

Cardinals

Chickadees

Crows

Juncos or snowbirds

Nuthatches

Tree Sparrows

Woodpeckers

Kinglets

Tree Buds

Maple—round and full

Beech—long and slender

Tulip—mitten shape

Buckeye—large and sticky

Appendix E. Examples of Memory Fireplace Rocks and Minerals

Indian Net Sinker or Banner Stone from Chagrin River Valley, Ohio

Brachiopods—marine shells—from Kelly's Island Ohio in Lake Erie

Natural Concrete—pebbles cemented by earth and water from Little Mountain, Ohio

White Coral

Flint from Flint Ridge Ohio

Fossil Coral from Kelly's Island Ohio in Lake Erie

Granite from the Mormon Temple, Salt Lake City, Utah

Granite from Mt Rushmore Memorial from Black Hills, South Dakota

Granite, "Rock of Ages," Barre, Vermont

Huron River shale—iron pyrite

Bog ore (iron ore) from iron ore furnace in Madison, Ohio

Igneous Rock Shot with Quartz brought by the Ice Age

Lava Rock from Carlsbad, New Mexico

Lava from Kiluae Volcano, Island of Hawaii.

Lead and Zinc from Rish Mine, Toho National Park, BC, Canada

Niagara Limestone scratched and scored as it was brought down by the Painesville (drift) in the Ice Age.

Salamanca Limestone from Buffalo, New York

Pegmatite from geological dyke, Lost River Nature Camp, Woodstock, New Hampshire (chosen by park naturalist)

Petrified wood—which is essentially quartz—from Arizona

Mass of Quartz from Seventh Lake, New York

Slag from iron ore furnace in Madison, Lake County, Ohio

Rocks from Mendenhall Glacier, Arkansas

Rocks from New Found Gap, Smoky Mountains, Tennessee

Appendix F. Museum Exhibits

There were 16 built-in cases (eight double-door) in the museum. When a "special" exhibit wasn't mounted, the cases contained:

Animals

Arrowheads

Birds (mounted)

Chimney Swift nest

Butterflies

Ferns

Fossil (in rock)

Fungi

Insects

Iron Ore

Lead Ore

Leaf specimens

Log cut by Beaver (eastern)

Log cut by Beaver (western)

Mushrooms (preserved)

Pine Cones

Pine Leaf Scale

Rocks (mounted)

Soil Specimens

Wasp's Nests

Wild Flowers

Wood studies (in box)

pictures

charts

maps

Leaf Press

Appendix G. Science Club Property in the Lodge

Furniture and Equipment–at cost: 12/31/1941

Adirondack chairs–12

Amplifier

Chairs–100

Cots–4

Cot Pads–4

Dishes

Enlarger

Green chairs–8

Fire extinguisher

Hose

Ladder

Lamp

Lawnmower

Loudspeaker

Motion picture projector

Oil Stove

Porch rug

Printing box

Range

Refrigerator

Rugs–2

Silverware

Stepladder

Tables–8

Telescope

Totem pole

Wheelbarrow

Total: $1321.33

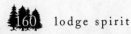

Appendix H. Anton Nosek's Other Metroparks Buildings

Buildings designed for Cleveland Metroparks, and which are still standing in 2009, include:

Building	Year Designed	Reservation[57]
Maple Grove Shelter		Rocky River
Forest Picnic Shelter	1933	North Chagrin
Lake Picnic Shelter	1934	Euclid Creek
Shelter House	1935	Huntington Park
Shelter House	1935	South Chagrin
Oak Grove Shelter	1935/36	Brecksville
Old River Farm Cookhouse[58]	1935/36	North Chagrin
River Grove Camp*	1938	North Chagrin

*(aka: American Legion Camp and Greater Cleveland YMCA River Road Camp)

Appendix I. Ellis Persing's Lodge Dedication Speech

The following excerpt is from Ellis Persing's Lodge dedication speech, given on June 5, 1938:

"For seven years, this club was without a regular meeting place. The School of Education and Public Library were available for lectures and business meetings. The trails and picnic grounds in the Metropolitan Park served for our out-door activities. However, we realized the disadvantage of not having a permanent headquarters.

"In bad weather it was frequently necessary to cancel the program and go home. Then too, the out-door schedule was limited to late spring, summer, and early autumn. Through the cooperation of the Metropolitan Park Director we solved our problems, at least for a time, by repairing the abandoned old farmhouse at the corner of Solon and River roads, and using the building as our headquarters. This structure was the original Look About Lodge.

"As the membership increased, the limited space at the old lodge was no longer adequate. It was difficult to seat adequately a group for a lecture or motion pictures, and then only about one-fifth of the membership could be accommodated at one time. The kitchen was too small. It would not permit us to have dinner meetings of the whole club.

"The museum idea was gaining interest but the room would not allow for enlarging it to meet the needs of the club. The out-door stove would serve about twenty-five to thirty people. In fact, we had completely outgrown the old building.

"About three years ago we began discussing plans for larger quarters. There seemed to be one of two courses to follow—remodel and enlarge the old lodge or erect a new building. I must confess, I favored a new building.

"I was encouraged to develop the idea by club members and friends. Briefly, we sold the idea to the club. Then, through the cooperation of the Metropolitan Park Board and WPA, we were able to break ground for this building on October 7 of last year.

"We had plans to build on the old site and I was very much in favor of it. But, one day, I had a call from Mr. Munson. He had tried to locate the building in the old location but it could not be placed to any advantage. Mr. Stinchcomb and Mr. Munson were agreed that this was a better site. So one rainy October evening the Executive Committee explored the present site. The decision was unanimously in favor of it. The next day ground was broken and building operations began. The advantages of this location are obvious.

"Several people have said to me, 'Our dream came true.' Yes! But to make this dream a reality we must not let our responsibility to the club cease. We must continue to serve the individual members and the community.

"This building has been designed for an extensive educational program. This room will seat about two hundred persons for lectures. During the summer months, another one hundred can be accommodated by using the long porch.

"The kitchen will be equipped to serve one hundred fifty or more for dinner meetings. The second floor is a reference room and museum. Here some members may carry out investigations and research. Others will enjoy it as a museum maintained by members of the club.

"In the museum the exhibits will be planned for the interpretation of both local and national areas, to show the history and development of science, to demonstrate arranging science materials for teaching units, and to stimulate and show the use of a museum for clubs.

"The south porch and the deck porch will serve for the smaller working group of fifteen or twenty people. The east porch is screened and can be used for larger committee meetings. Some of our committees range from fifteen to twenty-five persons—for example, the trail and museum committees.

"In the basement we have a modern heating plant. This makes the building available all year and I am inclined to believe you will want to use the Lodge in winter as well as summer. However, plans for the winter months are not definite. Adjoining the furnace room is a room, which will be used as a darkroom for the photographic group and as a general work room.

"The out-door stove and tables as a unit will accommodate about one hundred persons. Here a field group can have a program independent of the activities in the Main Building.

"The out-door lecture area, resembling an amphitheater, will seat about one hundred fifty persons. Here lectures, motion pictures, demonstrations, and campfire programs can be held during summer months.

"The building and grounds are none too large for the activities of two hundred and fifty members.

"It is true, we are interested in conservation; we desire to promote science in the schools. We do sponsor investigation and exploration. We encourage travel for background information and life enrichment. But there is one more way I am hoping this Lodge will serve us—

"It should be a place to which we may come to get away from the mad rush of the daily routine; a place where we may think undisturbed; a place where I can find myself. The quote by John Burrows over the north fireplace expresses this thought."

I come here often to find myself—
It is so easy to get lost in the world![59]

Other speakers at the Lodge dedication

Miss Helen Miller—CNSC President (presiding)

W. H. Cameron—Acting Director W.P.A.

Charles H. Lake—Superintendent of Cleveland Schools

Harold T. Clark—President, Cleveland
Museum of Natural History

Arthur Munson—Landscape Architect,
Metropolitan Park District

Harry N. Irwin—Dean, School of Education,
Western Reserve University

C. M. Shipman—President, Lake Erie Wild
Flower Club and Burroughs Nature Club

Homer Jewitt, President—Bird Club

J. Paul Visscher—Chairman, Department of
Biology, Western Reserve University

W. A. Stinchcomb—Executive Director-
Secretary, Cleveland Metropolitan Park Board

A stringed trio provided music before the
program and during the tea that followed.

Appendix J. Arthur L. Munson Excerpts

From the Fiftieth Anniversary Dinner Presentation Cleveland Metroparks Architect and Director. (The following excerpt is from remarks made about and by Mr. Munson.)

Arthur Munson played a prominent part in both the building of today's Look About Lodge, the educational programs offered by the Science Club, and development of Cleveland's Emerald Necklace. He was in many ways a benefactor of the Science Club.

He supervised the planting of trees, the building of roads, the layout of nature trails, and the construction of trailside museums. He was a member of the Science Club, plus the American Society of Landscape Architects, the Garden Center of Greater Cleveland, the Audubon Society, and the Burroughs Nature Club, among other civic groups.

Arthur Munson came to Cleveland after graduating from Cornell University and joined a firm of landscape architects. In 1924, he was named Cleveland City Forester, and two years later became the landscape architect for the Cleveland Metropolitan Park Board. In 1943, he was named Properties Director for the City of Cleveland.

In 1974, when the Science Club held its fiftieth anniversary, Arthur Munson was living in Colorado. The Club contacted his daughter who said he had been very ill and did not think it possible for him to attend.

When Arthur Munson heard about the anniversary, he was so delighted that he got out of bed and came to Cleveland a month before the celebration to rest up at his daughter's house and be ready to attend. He was there with his wife, daughter, and son-in-law. His comments at the anniversary dinner included the following:

He reiterated the story of the original Look About Lodge, and the Park Board's offer of a site for a new Lodge. "After considerable searching, Professor Persing and I selected the present site. Professor Persing learned that the Club would prefer a log building, so a search was begun for logs.

"We found them near Loudonville, Ohio, where there was sufficient native chestnut wood to construct the building. There were many problems to be worked out in constructing a building of this size, such as building the balcony, stairways, and the second floor.

"The quotations, carved in wood above the fireplaces by WPA artists, were suggested by Professor Persing and myself. 'I come here often to find myself...' from Burroughs was Professor Persing's selection, and I chose 'The life so short, the craft so long to learn' from Chaucer."

Grace Marriott was president of the Science Club during its fiftieth anniversary year. Her comments on Arthur Munson and Mr. Persing included:

"The good men do lives after them! All the good the past hath had remains to make our own time glad." She completed her remarks by pointing out, "We, you and I, are the recipients of that good. We are the beneficiaries and are very grateful to all those dedicated people who gave so much of themselves to 'make our own time glad.'"

Appendix K. Edward W. Doller Comments at the 50th Anniversary Dinner—Past President and Building Committee Member

"Our Program Chairman has suggested that my brief remarks pertain primarily to the building of the Lodge, so with few exceptions I will endeavor to comply.

"Those old enough to remember will recall the depression of 1929, which reached a peak in 1933 and continued with slight modification throughout the years 1934, 1935, and beyond. During this period, the government created various projects to help the unemployed such as the CCC, FERA, WPA, and PWA. It was also during this period that the Club accepted the Park Board's offer in September of 1931 to use the old Winslow house as its headquarters.

"Inspired by vacation trips to the western parks with rustic lodges, and the desire for more functional quarters for the Club, Mr. Persing frequently mentioned his dreams for the future. In June, 1935, dreams moved into reality when the (Parks) Board and the Club agreed jointly to the preparation of drawings for a new home.

"The architect hired was Anton George Nosek, or just plain Tony, who is now retired and living in California. (He has since passed away.) By August 12th, Tony had completed the bulk of

his work, and some of those drawings are here tonight for your inspection. On February 9, 1936, a letter was mailed to Mr. Stinchcomb stating that the Club had approved the drawings.

"What happened next is best described in Mr. Persing's original draft of his talk at the dedication ceremonies here in this room on June 5, 1938, in which he said, 'We had planned to build on the old site and I was personally very much in favor of it. But, one day, I had a telephone call from Mr. Munson. He informed me that they had tried to locate the building in the old location site but it could "not be placed to any advantage." Mr. Stinchcomb and Mr. Munson agreed that this was the best location for our building.'

"The balance of the year 1936 was presumably required by the Park Board to work out their arrangements with the government, because, as you know, three parties would be involved in the project.

"In October our Executive Committee visited the new sight and voiced their unanimous approval. During the late fall and winter, foundations were built. As members of the Building Committee, Fred Baker and I were seeking suitable logs, which he finally located in the vicinity of Loudonville, Ohio. After arrival here, the bark was removed with an adze. There were two originally which were mounted in this room. After their mysterious disappearance, they were replaced with others which bear some resemblance to the originals.

"Labor employed on the project was classified as Unskilled, Intermediate, Skilled, and Technical or Superintendence. Many of the men were so proud of their opportunity to share in the construction that they brought their families out on Sundays to watch the building take form.

"When it came to the roof, it was quite evident to most of us that a colorful modern covering would detract from the rustic plan so far created. Furthermore, we were forever cost conscious. The Park Board solved the problem by locating some used slate which at some time must have been coated with tar or the equivalent. Much of this still clung to the slate whiled the roofers nailed it in place.

"After the outside of the building had received a coat of preservative, it harmonized as much with its environment thirty-five years ago as it does today. Inside this room, these untouched logs still convey to those inspired by things natural, a feeling which is sometimes difficult to describe. It is the way Ellis and Jennie Persing and all who were involved wanted them, and we hope they will always remain that way.

"For a few years after completion of the building, it was interesting to observe during our annual housekeeping that minute forms of life were presumably still active in the wood as evidenced by tiny mounds of powdery dust along the top surface of some logs. Ultimately, this action ceased.

"With respect to the newel posts at the foot of the two north stairways, I have a feeling of guilt. One of the workmen who was talented as a wood carver had very effectively fastened a chain around one post, and I believe there was something different on the other. Mr. Persing and I both admired the creation, but finally agreed that the carvings were neither relevant nor in harmony with the simplicity of the stairways. Ultimately, removal of the carvings was authorized, and my conscience still bothers me for being partially responsible for the final decision.

"Mr. Stinchcomb took a keen interest in the preliminary as well as the final drawings of the lodge. In the beginning, only two stairways were included on the east side of the room. Later the plans were changed to one in each corner. During one of his visits, Mr. Stinchcomb said, 'Why four stairways? In place of the one in the southeast corner, how about a book nook with shelves and a window seat?' So a book nook it is. For several years after completion, Mr. Stinchcomb carried a key to the main entrance so he might with considerable pride bring out-of-town visitors and others to see this unusual structure.

"This room measures sixty-one by twenty-six feet. Overall length of the building from the north wall of the kitchen to the edge of the south porch is approximately ninety-five feet. The screened porch adds approximately twelve feet to the overall width totaling about thirty-eight feet. Other items of interest in this room and elsewhere about the building are the lighting fixtures which were made in the barn that stands on the reservation near Cannon Road. (It is no longer there.)

"Tony Nosek's drawings called for a central heating system with a furnace located in the basement. Estimates Fred Baker obtained soon after the construction had begun now indicated a probably need within sixty days for an additional six hundred dollars over budget. It was then that some of us envisioned a couple of base burners placed in this room in conjunction with the fireplaces.

"But most clouds have a silver lining—in this case, on the person of Norman Hurst, then superintendent of the Metropark's Eastern Division. Norman convinced us how pennywise and pound foolish it would be to forego the use of WPA labor to install the ducts at no cost to the Club.

"He then mentioned Mr. Forrest Fram who operated a business in Chagrin Falls which specialized in heating equipment and installations. The Fram bid enabled us to proceed with the central system. Incidentally, Mr. Fram is retired and still resides in Chagrin with his wife who operates the Brass Shoppe at 512 Washington Street.

"Years later, when the coal burning furnace was in need of major repairs, the responsibility for conversion to oil was accepted by a most capable past member, George Inman.

"A beautiful building without an ample supply of good water would have been disastrous, but again we were fortunate. Relying on memory, I believe the well drilling at the northwest corner of the building descended sixty feet.

"A Myers pump of three gallons per minute capacity manufactured in Ashland, Ohio, was installed and is still in service. Tests of the water made occasionally by the City of Cleveland showed water of exceptional purity for drinking.

"Without access to any pre-established sewage system, disposal of liquid waste from the kitchen together with the effluent form the inside toilet facilities and floor drains had to be handled in the properly prescribed manner. This necessitated a piping layout below the basement floor level, which exited the building and continued down the hill to the northeast for a considerable distance to a septic tank.

"As you all know, the (Park) Board granted the Club's desire for a picnic location in a wooded area convenient to the Lodge, with a four way fireplace and ample table capacity. However, everyone here may not have been acquainted with the outdoor lecture area just beyond the picnic location.

"It was equipped with logs neatly arranged for seating. It also had a speaker's rostrum and a large wooden projection board on which slides and movies could be shown. Unfortunately, during the mosquito season, it was unbearable to use the area from early evening on, so nature was permitted to gradually reclaim it.

"When reminiscing, as I have done, it is easy to overdo. One thing leads to another, and I could continue. It seems appropriate to stop with this thought: Without the impelling urge and enthusiasm behind Mr. Persing's dreams, where might we be tonight?"

Appendix L. Background Reference Sources

Many of the documents gathered during this effort have been digitized for future reference. They are available to anyone interested in this special piece of Greater Cleveland's history. The originals will be given to the Western Reserve Historical Society for safekeeping.

Source documents include early newsletters and photos saved in scrapbooks by Club members over the years, including notes from Ellis C. Persing.

Books

A dated, but still valid, list of "chestnut"[60] nature influences includes:

Cleveland Metroparks: Past and Present; Celebrating 75 Years of Conservation, Education, and Recreation 1917 to 1992; by Carol Poh Miller.

Paddle to the Sea by Holling C. Holling; 1941; Houghton Mifflin Company; A Caldecott Honor Book in 1942.

Sajo and the Beaver People by Grey Owl; Charles Scribner's Sons; © 1936

Wild Animals I have Known by Ernest Thompson Seton; 1898;

Lives of the Hunted by Ernest Thompson Seton;

The Travels of William Bartram.

Two Little Savages, Being the Adventures of Two Boys Who Lived as Indians and What They Learned; (twelve-year-old boys) with over two hundred drawings, by Ernest Thompson Seton; © 1903; Doubleday Page & Company, New York

A more contemporary list of nature influences and references includes:

Brother Wolf: A Forgotten Promise by Jim Brandenburg; Northword Press; 1997.

Last Child In The Woods; Saving Our Children from Nature-Deficit Disorder, by Richard Louv; Algonquin Books of Chapel Hill; 2005.

Wolf Walking—by Edwin Daniels and Judi Rideout; Stewart, Tabori, and Chang; New York, 1997.

Cleveland Metroparks—*Past and Present, Celebrating 75 years...* Carol Poh Miller; Cleveland Metroparks Cleveland OH; 1992.

Cleveland Metroparks—*Images of America Series*; Thomas G. Matowitz; Arcadia Publishing; San Francisco CA; 2006

Numerous Bulletins and ByPaths, newsletters of the Cleveland Natural Science Club, and other CNSC historical records such as the Annual Reports to the Metroparks Directors.

Websites

http://www.ecotopia.org/

http://en.wikipedia.org/wiki/John_Bartram

http://www.audubon.org/nas/jja.html

http://www.audubon.org

http://www.pbs.org/wnet/americanmasters/episodes/john-james-audubon/career-timeline/107/

http://www.pbs.org/wnet/americanmasters/episodes/john-james-audubon/career-timeline/107/

http://www.sierraclub.org/john_muir_exhibit/life/chronology.aspx

http://www.yosemite.org/visitor/frequent-cultural.htm

http://www.etsetoninstitute.org

http://www.aloveoflearning.org/ernest_thompson_seton

http://www.etsetoninstitute.org/

http://nobelprize.org/nobel_prizes/peace/laureates/1906roosevelt-bio.html

http://www.nps.gov/history/history/hisnps/index.htm

http://en.wikipedia.org/wiki/Antiquities_Act–cite_note-0

Other

From CNSC Historical filesPaper on the history of the Lodge by Adelaide Lennie Snider, written on May 18, 1974. Adelaide joined the Science Club in 1938.

Paper on the history of the Lodge by Ann Burgess, written on September 21st, 1963.

Paper by Grace Marriott, president 1975/76/77.

Appendix M. Photo Credits

A number of the photos were from the Science Club historical files, with the photographer unknown. Those whose sources are known include the following:

Page 15, 20, 21, 22, 93, 99 (doorbell), 104, 106 (kitchen), 123: author

Page 60: Cleveland Metroparks

Page 75: Ellis Persing, Jr.

Page 99 (front door light), 100, 101, 102, 103, 105, 137: Sandra M. Cobb

Endnotes

1 Pronounced Dōllĕr.

2 A very attractive post binder scrapbook used to catalog many documents was purchased at The Higbee Company for 75 cents. (Probably purchased in the 1930s)

3 One folder in the CNSC history files (evidentially from a teacher) was labeled in beautiful script handwriting, "Physical Science."

4 When Ralph Kneale (Sr.) was a Club Trustee (1974-1975)

5 Popular American essayist and nature writer during the late 1800's. See Chapter II.

6 "*Last Child In The Woods; Saving Our Children from Nature-Deficit Disorder*," by Richard Louv; Algonquin Books of Chapel Hill; 2005

7 By Ernest Thompson Seton.

8 Brother Wolf: A Forgotten Promise" by Jim Brandenburg; November, 1993.

9 By this time, my wife and I were in our 60s.

10 http://ech.case.edu/ech-cgi/article.pl?id=EUMC.

11 Go to www.cleveland.com/universitycircleguide/

12 Although Ellis Persing's Lodge dedication speech didn't mention Epworth, records do show that the group met there.

13 The Great Depression began with the stock market crash on *Black Friday*, October 29, 1929.

14 Works Progress Administration created by the government to gainfully employ workers during the Great Depression.

15 An area which covers much of Northeast Ohio, and which was originally a set-aside for the state of Connecticut.

16 Kingdom, Phylum, Class, Order, Family, Genius, Species—to be remembered by "King Philip Came Over From Greater Spain.

17 From Wikipedia, the free encyclopedia

18 for more information, go to Bartrams garden.org.

19 http://www.fieldtrip.com/pa/06665593.htm

20 http://www.pbs.org/wnet/americanmasters/episodes/john-james-audubon/drawn-from-nature/106/

21 An animal employing vivipary: the embryo develops inside the body of the mother, as opposed to outside in an egg.

22 http://ecotopia.org/ecology-hall-of-fame/john-burroughs/

23 http://www.americanheritage.com/articles/magazine/ah/1971/2/1971_2_60.shtml

24 Brainyquote web site, http://www.brainyquote.com/quotes/authors/j/john_burroughs.html

http://www.johnburroughs.org

25 PBS: The American Experience;

http://www.pbs.org/wgbh/amex/1900/filmmore/transcript/transcript1.html

26 Pronounced "Het Hetchy"

27 First broadcast on PBS in 2008.

28 © Philmont Museum and Seton Memorial Library

29 Selected by William McKinley as a compromise, Theodore Roosevelt was not considered to be a *presidential* material.

30 See: http://www.theodoreroosevelt.org/

31 http://www.americanheritage.com/articles/magazine/ah/1971/2/1971_2_60.shtml

32 http://www.nps.gov/history/history/hisnps/index.htm

33 One problem is that the records of the time reveal that the idea of a national park had been proposed some years before 1870. In addition, there are only four known diaries of the expedition and none of these mentions the campfire conversation.

34 Renown wildlife movie director, who did a series on America's national parks, aired in the fall of 2009.

35 http://encyclopedia2.thefreedictionary.com, compiled by William Robert Johnston.

36 When The Wolves Returned by Dorothy Hinshaw Patent; Walker and Company, New Yrok, 2008. as well as other books listed in Appendix F, Background Reference Sources.

37 http://en.wikipedia.org/wiki/Environmental_movement

38 Cleveland Metroparks: Past and Present; Celebrating 75 Years of Conservation, Education, and Recreation 1917 to 1992; by Carol Poh Miller.

39 From an article in the Cleveland Plain Dealer on April 25, 1932; written by: Edna K. Wooley, Cleveland Plain Dealer Reporter and Cleveland Natural Science Club Member.

40 The Western Reserve University professor who inspired Education College alumni to found the Cleveland Natural Science Club.

41 Cleveland's morning newspaper.

42 An east side shopping area.

43 A downtown department store in Cleveland's Terminal Tower.

44 *Charles H. Kettering*, American inventor, businessman, and research engineer. Kettering held over 300 patents[1]. He was a founder of Delco, and headed General Motors research efforts for 27 years from 1920 to 1947.

45 An afternoon daily newspaper. She apparently moved there from The Plain Dealer.

(see page 107)

46 Anton Nosek's parents were from Vienna, although he was born in the US

47 The Cleveland Natural Science Club Bulletin; January 7, 1938.

48 From the National List of Historic Places application; 2007

49 A Cleveland afternoon newspaper.

50 This was the college which provided evening and weekend classes for part-time students.

51 http://www.amazon.co.uk/Elementary-science-grades-nature-reader/dp/B001FT9IEE/ref=sr_1_2/276-0260586-9189029?ie=UTF 8&s=books&qid=1248021974&sr=1-2

52 http://www.ecotopia.org/ehof/timeline.html

53

54 Cleveland Metroparks: Past and Present; Celebrating 75 Years of Conservation, Education, and Recreation 1917 to 1992; by Carol Poh Miller.

55

56 Historic Register Information in this section was compiled by Wendy Weirich, Look About Lodge Naturalist Manager and Sandy Cobb, MLS, Cleveland Metroparks Volunteer. Historical data, and memories, were provided by Ralph M. Kneale, Jr. whose parents were Club members beginning in 1938.

57 in 2006

58 Anton Nosek designed a number of cookhouses from a basic design appropriate for all Cleveland Metroparks Reservations.

59 John Burrows; American Essayist (1837–1921); a popular nature writer in his time, due to his "simple values, simple means, simple ends" writing style.

60 Librarians—and others in the "book" industry—call old volumes "chestnuts."

61 Given to me for Christmas in 1942 by my surrogate aunt (see page 10).

62 Brother Wolf: A Forgotten Promise" by Jim Brandenburg; November, 1993.